to Elsie

My favorite student

Richard A Maryanski

Antique Picture Frame Guide

By

Richard A. Maryanski, Ph.B.

Edited by

Anne Lunde

Published by Cedar Forest Co., 7316 N. Milwaukee Avenue, Niles, Illinois 60648
Printed by Hewitt Bros., Niles, Illinois

Introduction

The purpose of this book is to give a comprehensive study of the development of the picture frame from the beginning of its existence to the picture frame of today. The book will dwell upon the early aspects of framing, when the picture frame grew from nothing more than a border around a picture. The section dealing with Pre-Revolutionary period will attempt to show the gradual development of frames, including their origin, characteristics, and how they blossomed with time as a result of the fruits of man's labor and feelings. The Post-Revolutionary section deals with the the development of the frame as it is related to America, while the Pre-Civil War section centers around the development of the frame before the Civil War.

Since the picture frame is a manufactured item, its development is directly related to the development of American industry. As industry grew, so did the development of the picture frame. While much of the skill in the making came from Europe, the mass production technique was developed in America.

This may well be the first time that information pertaining to the picture frame and its technical development has been assembled in one book. The frames exhibited and the information set forth in this book are the result of twelve years of work in seeking and restoring antique picture frames. There are comparatively few, if any, books written on the subject of antique picture frames. Much of the knowledge of frames has been collected from persons who had actual experience in working with frames, either in the manufacture or the sales of frames.

Information was also secured by actually working with old frames. Much of it came from what was behind the picture in the frame. Newspapers, for example, give dates which can indicate the approximate period of the frames manufacture. These dates along with a gradual development of the design change, show when a certain type of frame appeared and disappeared, and in time, the step by step development of the frame becomes clear.

Physical information regarding to composition, cutting and assembly, and related items of a picture such as nails, glass, etc, will be discussed to give a more complete story of the frame. The composition of the picture frame is better understood when one is familiar with the vital, pertinent information under discussion.

Still another object of this book is to show how big manufacturers have attemped to gain sales from one another by lowering production costs. By this something was lost. The development of the oval frame is an example of this loss. While we discuss the early beginnings of related items of picture frames, the main emphasis of the book will be the period between 1800 to 1910. The majority of people interested in antique frames today will in all probability, have some of this period or at least can get them.

Frames of the 13th century are almost unobtainable and it is fruitless to discuss at a great length a commodity that you can only occasionally see in an art museum. Because the subject of gold leaf and other leafing materials is one that many people who are interested in picture frames know little about, the book attempts to give a comprehensive picture of leaf and its relationship to picture framing. Technical aspects such as the types of wood and the methods of finishing frames will be also discussed.

Various problems relating to the restoration of the antique frame are covered, because this information is of great interest to individuals who collect or use antique frames. There will be ample information covering the most common problems that one comes across when working with these frames. The trends of picture framing today will be discussed as well as the use of the antique frame in the home, and what types of frames that would be utilized for the various motifs and periods.

Finally, with a basic study of how frames are distributed today along with the basic purchasing structure of the suppliers and antique dealers will be discussed. The book shows how to prevent further damage to existing antique frames and endeavors to convey a different sense of appreciation to these things of beauty which are going out of existence. It is hoped that from reading this book, the reader will have attained one thing, a feeling for the old, for what had been accomplished by man through the use of his hands and his mind. The antique picture frame is an example of what man could do when he had to, or better still, when he wanted to. Many of the skills involved in these beautiful frames will never be perpetrated again. They will go the way of the passenger pigeon; to be remembered but never to be created again.

Dedication

I wish to dedicate this book to my mother Camille Maryanski, whose faith in me has been endless, to my wife Chloe Z. Maryanski, who has helped and encouraged me in my endeavor, and finally a special thanks to my son Jim Maryanski for his invaluable assistance.

Acknowledgements

In the immediate preparation of this book I want to express my appreciation to those that have offered their assistance: The Art Institute of Chicago, Vilas-Mages Company, Grace Lunde, Walter Larsen and Norman Klenz.

Most of the frames shown are from the Jonas Tobiason Collection.

Table of Contents

Left Figure A

Italian school. 1550, Virgin and Child, frame is intricately fitted of wood forming columns and head pieces, all red clay covered and gold leaf applied. Courtesy Art Institute, Chicago.

Right Figure B

Jacobi De Cioni, Madonna and Child. 1365-1398. Italian, wood carved, gold leaf applied, wood spirals that were turned. Courtesy Art Institute, Chicago.

Left Figure C

Fransesco Botticini, Italian, 1446-1498. Virgin and Child with two Angels, very intricate carving, typical column effect of the period. Courtesy Art Institute, Chicago.

I — The Pre-Revolutionary Period

For prehistoric man, there were no frames to be used for his creations. The early drawings by primitive man were on the walls of caves and on items of use. These creations were painted on walls, perhaps to relate a story, or else on vases and other implements. They were used to decorate many objects. The human form with its true form in perspective was to come later. The Egyptian drawings depicted stories, but the forms are primitive and unorthodox by today's standards. Art developed as time went on through periods of continual change. That eventually led to the basis of what is accepted as art today. This gradual progression of art covered many centuries. Practically all the art was applied to surfaces that were either of a fixed proportion or items of use. The portable picture was to come later.

The church was to provide the dominant influence in art for centuries because it had a story to relate. As artists sought to express the truth of God and their religion, art developed into a truer more correct perspective. Painting was done on the walls of churches, the ceilings and the insets about the church. They were to be bordered to an extent by a framing unit This was not a movable item. Instead, it was constructed and elaborated as part of the church.

With the passing of time, there began to appear a simple border around the painting, which was actually integrated with the picture. The frame was textured and joined to the picture by the use of glue and chalk. Eventually the frame was emphasized and became a separate item.

The first true frame was a wood frame of the simplest design. This frame later developed with time and carvings and other decorations began to be added. Eventually the frames were given a prominent place in the structure of the picture unit. The frames reflected on the decor of the church with spirals and embellishments similar to those used on the steeples. (Figures A, B, C, D, E) Carving began to be more intricate and flowers, petals, scrolls, leaves, and geometric designs began to appear in the carvings.

In Italy the frames began to blossom with design, and France soon adopted the same idea. Michelangelo's "Holy Family" has a fine round frame. Created by Antonio Barile, it is completely hand carved with five protruding human heads. This work is a fine example of the type of frame that adorned the early Italian paintings.

Most of the existing works of art of this period are of a religious nature. Religion brought forth the aesthetic feelings of the artists. The artist of that day expressed his inner feelings, his emotions love, affection, and his symbolism of tranquility in life. The artists of today have the same feeling. They see before them the world as it is, but in their paintings, they try to symbolize the same feelings of love, emotion, etc. No one on earth can say that is wrong.

In the era from 1550 to about 1630 there emerged an Italian three-piece frame that was to become the dominant type for the most part until the beginning of the eighteenth century. (Figures K, L). The frame consisted of a fluted inner liner, a second frame that was flat with embossing or treated with some design, and finally an outer frame that could be designed like the inner liner or with some other variation. Raphael's "Madonna and Child" is adorned with this type of frame. Variations of this basic frame were to predominate during the 16th century.

From the comparatively flat design of the early 16th century more relief designs evolved and with more of a heavier feeling. A gradual change in the 17th century brought designs, still delicate and light, but with larger and higher relief. There were more foliate reliefs (Figure M) and new forms were being developed. Carvings were becoming bolder in body.

Paulo Veneziano, Italian, 1333-1358, St. Augustine, St. Peter, St. Catherine of Alexandria, St. John the Baptist, wood carved and leafed, typical frame of the period, Italian. Courtesy Art Institute, Chicago.

Right Figure E

Judgment of Paris, 1536, delicate wood carving, red clay base, gold leaf, intricate undercut carving. Courtesy Art Institute, Chicago.

Left Figure F

Fredrick T. Haskell Coll. 1550, wood carved, tortoise shell inlay, gold leaf impressed decor. Courtesy Art Institute, Chicago.

The picture frame was developing into an important part of the picture unit instead of just a housing for it.

The Renaissance period (14th-17th centuries) was a time of awakening throughout Europe. It was as if a giant, asleep for the centuries through the Dark ages and Middle ages, suddenly awoke. The woven band of power built up by the church along with its continual abuses was to receive new thought and new attentions that started a movement of reformation. Before this, the Middle ages was a period of almost no experimentation or scientific advances. The continent seemed to move in circular wanderings with constant fighting between many little kingdoms, yet gradual consolidations, as in the German and French provinces, did appear. The tempo in art was for the most part crude, as the arts were not being developed, and there was a barbaric influence from the tribes of the northern wilderness or beyond the mountains of the western section of Asia.

The years between 1400-1600 were to see the Renaissance period expand the arts to a height never before reached. Paintings played an important part in this period. Da Vinci, Raphael, and Michelangelo were just a few of the many artists to come from this period. Italy fostered the revival of art, architecture and designing with France closely following her.

Renaissance art was encouraged by Frances I, who brought many of the Italian craftsmen to France. The influence of the artisans was present in the frames that were later to come from that country. The French influence developed into a separate style that was to show up later when two recognizable schools of frames developed as time went on: the Italian and the French.

By the 16th century, the frame was considered as much a piece of furniture as the mirror and as much a part of the interior of a building as wall decorations or panels were. Many fine frames were later to evolve from the reign of Louis XIII (1610-1643). The effects of the importation of work by the Italian artisans by Francis I were to show up in the French frames of the period that were the French interpretations of the Italian type of frame. The French developed their own type of frame full of flowing lines. They used continuous patterns such as the egg and dart ribbon, and a profusion of leaves and foliage intertwined together. The ribbon effect was carved to seem to leave the frame in dimension and then flow back to it. This involved a considerable undercutting of the pattern. These patterns continued to the end of the 18th century and even today, some of the patterns are used in cylindrical compo work.

During the reign of Louis XIV of France, this gradual change of French style continued and toward the end of his reign, there was a definite new character to the French type of frames.

The Dutch influence in the 16th century had a completely different school of interpretation for picture frames. The Dutch with a great sphere of trade in the world, had access to many fine woods which were used profusely in the creations by the Dutch masters of that period. Ebony, oak, walnut, fruitwood, and exotic woods were used for the frames. The frame was at times carved but in a subdued way. The use of gold trim was very limited when it was used at all. The color black was extensively used as well as the other subdued dark colors. Frames were considered to be bold and direct, with no glaring attraction of attention to the frame itself. This was in direct opposition to the French frames of that era. Much of the background of the Dutch painters was very dark and this darkness fused to the dark colors of the frame. At times, many of the frames were rich in carved detail but they were always subdued by the dark color. (Figure I)

Sumptuous frames were to reach a new high during the reign of Louis XV, (1723-1774). In this glorious and decadent period frames were created to adorn the palaces with the finest of creations man could devise. Fireplace screens were framed, wall paneling was framed, and flamboyant

Left Figure G

Jan Van Hemessen, Dutch, 1550-1575, titled Judith, wood carved leaves separately applied and gesso covered, gold leaf finish. Courtesy Art Institute, Chicago.

Right Figure H

Flemish, 1610-1690, hand carved ebony wood, frame black with no gold tone, typical Dutch influence frame. Courtesy Art Institute, Chicago.

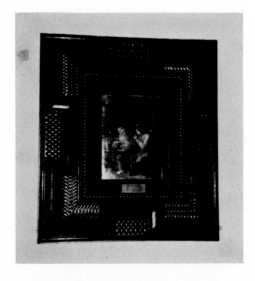

Left Figure I

Quentin Massys, Flemish, 1465-1530. Man with a Pink, Wood carved ebony, black finish, light gold tone on edges. Courtesy Art Institute, Chicago.

mirrors with flowing ribbons and foliage were prevalent in this era. This mode became an important element in the development of the Rococo style which is well known today. (Figure M) This type of frame exists today in a much modified form because it simply costs too much to create it as it was done in 1750. The artisans able to do this work today are very few.

Things were beginning to change when Louis XVI took the throne. There was a retreat to a more delicate filigree design and beading. The flamboyancy simmered down and the Barbizon type of frame made its appearance.

This frame exhibits the delicate filigree type of design on a curved surface with proper corner embellishments and a beading or similar edging. The effect is a subdued frame in contrast to the Rococo style which has protruding, flowing designs in graceful contours. There was more relief to the Rococo frame because of its protrusions.

The Barbizon frame, considered to be an imitation of the Louis XIV frames, had considerable detail in flowing lines, more or less flattened to a surface rather than flowing in dimension from the frame. The use of compo molds enabled the artisans of that period to keep up with the demand for a decorative frame that had the appearance of being carved from wood like many of the Rococo frames at the time. During the 19th century, the Barbizon frame was the dominant frame. It soon found its way to the United States by way of the immigrants who brought their skills and belongings with them. Figures O, J, 24, 36 and 74 are examples of the Barbizon frame.

Throughout most of Europe there were few new developments in frames during the 19th century. There were, however, changes appearing in the types of frames made in America. It was the home of the primitive frame, many of which housed early colonial primitive paintings.

America was to create many different types of frames. Examples of these are the combination oak and gold frame, (Figure 17), the American ovals, which were of a different treatment than the European oval styles which leaned toward the baroque, (Figure 36), along with velvet, wood and gold combinations, (Figure 105). There were many other variations which were definitely American in origin.

While it is true that Europe originated the compo design, there was little change in the designs. The variations in the way the Americans used them made the difference. Europe remained more or less in a rut in the field or design, but America experimented. Because of its ingenuity in developing mass production, it was able to create many different types of frames. European compo stick moulding was to remain with the basic designs developed during the 16th, 17th and the 18th centuries.

America depended on two basic sources of moulding in the 19th century. The first was the stick moulding that Europe had to offer along with the finished frames that Europe did produce at the turn of the century. The second was the stick moulding that primitive America and its small woodworking shops were able to produce at that time. With these two sources, all of the frames used in America were made.

Some of the fine, framed pictures in the museums today are not in the original frames used when they were first created, because throughout the ages there were changes to the framing indicative of the taste and the decor of that time. The old frame would be replaced for one reason or another so one cannot immediately make a judgment that the framing of a painting is representative of the typical style of the original time when it was painted.

Left Figure J

Paul Cezanne, French, 1839-1906. Madame Cezanne in yellow chair, Barbizon style compo mold applied with gold leaf. Courtesy Art Institute, Chicago.

Right Figure K

Italian Florence, 16th century. Portrait of a Woman, hand carved of walnut, the gilded note triple frame effect. Courtesy Art Institute, Chicago.

Left Figure L

Fransisco Guardi, Italian, 1912-1793, wood carved and gilted with gold leaf, center section simulated tortoise shell. Courtesy Art Institute, Chicago.

II – The Post-Revolutionary Period

Prior to the Revolutionary War, and for some time afterwards, practically all frames were imported to America from England, France, and Italy. England shipped the largest number and their frames had a distinctive style to their mouldings. On the other hand, France and Italy had very baroque frames with a considerable amount of carving and much detail. At the same time they were very expensive.

Stick moulding is the term applied to a 10 to 14 foot strip of picture frame moulding. The very fancy styles with much detail and width came from Europe. America now produces a limited amount of stick moulding but its production is nowheres near the demand.

Some of the English mouldings consisted of fine detail moulding that could be called a "tailored" fine detail. Also predominant in the English style of moulding was a maple veneer type of moulding, which is a veneer of maple glued to a suitable wood. Much of the framing material in the Revolutionary period was this type.

Simulated mahogany wood grain on a 1½ inch frame with a gold leaf lip was also used. This early style of frame must not be confused with a later design used until about 1910. The early frame had a simulated mahogany grain going with the grain of the wood and a superb gold leaf lip. The side was basically unfinished in the earlier frame and the graining was vague and not pronounced. The later frame had a more pronounced graining and there was some drop in the quality of the gold lip.

The frame that was pronounced around the period of 1890-1910 had a gilt finished lip, with the graining going perpendicular to the moulding. The sides were finished in black, and the nails were obvious with large heads. This change in quality was the evident result of cutting labor costs to produce a product.

A particularly fine piece of framing was a plain, but brilliant gold leaf frame of simple design. The gold leaf was burnished to a fine metallic finish. Sometimes a printed design was overlaid on its surface. One characteristic feature of this moulding was that the sides were for the most part unfinished. This type of frame lends itself perfectly for framing primitives.

Still another type was a mottled finish moulding. (Figure 1). Some had a stipple effect, while others had a pearly swirl effect. It must be kept in mind that this finish was not only used in the late 1700's, but also up to 1898 or so. This finish and its gradual expansion we shall call tortoise shell or modified tortoise finish. It formed the basis of many frame finishes that were to come later.

The maple veneer frame, (Figure 13) was one of the first to be duplicated here in America. To create a maple veneer frame, two things are needed. The first is a machine that can cut a veneer and the second is a shaped moulding to put the veneer on. Much of the moulding that contained contours were created by special planes with a design blade that would gradually give a contour on the wood by the process of planing back and forth until the desired design was formed. In this way a lip could be formed and many step designs were planed out of the wood. The wood worker would have to work on rather short pieces of wood because it was being hand planed and formed. All of the planes consisted of wood with the blade held in place by a wedge. This tool goes back a considerable period and it was developed during the time when most tools came into being. It was a matter of time before a shaper head was used and in the beginning it was powered by water or steam.

During the Revolutionary period, young America was an agricultural nation. We exported molasses, turpentine, lumber, furs, etc, and then imported finished goods including picture frames. Some of the lumber

Left Figure M

Antonio Allegreti, Italian, 1712-1793, Madonna and Child and St. John the Baptist intricate flowing lines almost Rococo in style except heavier in feeling, wood carved and leafed. Courtesy Art Institute, Chicago.

Right Figure N

Frans Pourbus the Younger, Flemish, 1569-1622. Portrait of Marie De Medici, wood carved and gold leafed, Flemish. Courtesy Art Institute, Chicago.

Left Figure O

Eugene Dela Croix, French, 1798-1863. Barbizon type, applied compo, gold leaf finish, typical French frame of the period. Courtesy Art Institute, Chicago.

which we exported would come back to us as moulding.

In order to fully understand what it took to create moulding, one has to consider what is needed to manufacture it: First, power was needed. At the time, the only source of power was water and steam power. Second, cutting tools were needed to form the wood frame design. They did not have carbide-tipped tools or high grade tungsten steel. The cutting or shaper heads that they had were of iron or early steel that required continual sharpening. This continual sharpening also reduced the shaper head specifications so that the quality control was difficult.

In the Post-Revolutionary period there were no factories to produce moulding. Eventually in the early 1800's, enterprising America began its step toward industrialization and at the same time, began to manufacture frames.

III — The Pre-Civil War Period

While the baroque frame with its finished corners was still being imported from Europe as well as heavy moulding, small wood shops began to emerge in America which crudely manufactured picture frames.

Fancy European moulding required over 28 individual steps from the unprepared wood to the finished item. Each step required hand motion, and it takes virtually the same steps today! Take a look at (Figure 24) and see how many individual manual steps were needed.

First came the cutting of the raw wood, and then planing to produce the finished stock. The next step was the routing to produce a tongue and groove edge in order to join two pieces of wood and to give the required form. Then came the routing of this form to obtain the desired shape of the moulding. This could involve three or more steps in routing. The sanding of this form came after that. Now the raw moulding is formed to take the desired finish or the application of compo for dimensional trim.

In the case of Figure 14, the surface application was in the form of paint finishes. First, an application of whiting paste was applied to the moulding. By pushing the raw moulding through a prepared form and then coating it with the whiting, a smooth surface resulted suitable for the first finish. After the drying, a prime coat was applied, sanded, and then another coat applied, which was also sanded by hand. In the case of a gold lip, a third coat would be applied, and then hand sanded and sealed with shellac and finally sanded again. Next, the gold size was applied and allowed to set and dry a certain time. Care had to be taken to edge the moulding exactly or a sloppy edge will result. Where the sizing is applied, the gold leaf will adhere. After applicatian of the leaf, the surface was sealed with shellac. Finally, a varnish application was needed to protect the very thin gold leaf application.

Various paint finishes are involved in this frame, each requiring separate steps. The sides are black in color. This is done by coating the sides with a flat black paint. The geometric design on the inside was created by applying a base coat of paint just to the area and then pressing a design on the surface by means of a printing wheel. The black edge is then hand stripped. To create a simulated wood finish a base coat is applied, then sanded. By means of a brush and other equipment a simulated wood finish is hand applied. The final finish is sealed and hand rubbed. All these stages were required to produce this moulding and to an extent many of these steps are still needed today to make some of the mouldings available.

Today, ways have been found to simulate some of the finishes. Sometimes a gold-colored aluminum foil is used to replace the gold lip. Milar,

Figure 1

Circa 1870
size 8 by 10
Mottled tortoise with black edging burnished gold lip, deep and large

Figure 2

Circa 1875
size 8 by 10
Gold edge black ebony with carving designed corners burnished gold lip

Figure 3

Circa 1870
size 10 by 12
Silver leaf three frame design Individual
compo trim

Figure 4

Circa 1875
size 8 by 10
Multicolor tortoise feather design touch of
blue added, four frames, hand carving on
sides and corners

Figure 5

Circa 1880
size 8 by 10
Known as the New York Frame
Four frame design, black with speckle tour-
toise, burnished gold liner, carved outer
edge

which is a plastic, can also be used for this purpose. Printed paper is being used to duplicate the wood grain and machines can mechanically stripe the moulding.

In the early 1800's the small woodwork shops were limited in what they could produce. At first they tried to reproduce what was being imported. After all, what better teaching material was there than what was already being made. We imitated as best as we could.

One of the biggest aids to picture frame manufacturing was the compo molds, (Figure 38). Practically all the ornate mouldings were created by molds of some form. There is a fallacy that all of the ornate trim on picture frames was hand carved. But even then there was a labor cost, and the thought that someone would sit and carve all that moulding, inch by inch, and yet sell it for a few dollars is absurd. This is not to say that frames were never hand carved because there did exist hand carved frames, although they were few in comparison. Most early European frames were intricately carved and then dipped in whiting and eventually gold-leaved. All of the frames of Italian and French origin dating back to Michael-angelo's time were done in this manner. Obviously, if one went back far enough, one could assume that once they were all hand carved.

In Europe, when one went to get a custom frame, he really got a custom frame, (Figure 27). Artists generally did not pay much attention to standard sizes. The result was usually odd sizes in paintings. In the early days the artist would take his creation measuring, for example, 37¾ inches by 41½ inches to the framer and say, "make a frame". The framer really created a frame, complete with finished corners. He would create molds to mold the various trim involved and hand contour the base frame into which these parts would be fitted.

The early molds consisted of two forms. The first was hand carved out of dogwood, maple or other hard woods with little grain. Today this would fall into the category of tool and die work. The average mold today would each cost five to eight hundred dollars to produce. (Figure 38) is an example of the various hand carved molds.

The other form of molds consisted of a piece of heavy wood with a cavity carved out of it, (Figure 38, center mold). Into the cavity a hot tar and sulfur compound was poured. The carved section to be used was then pressed into the molten mixture and allowed to cool. When it cooled, the carved section was removed and a mold was produced.

In order to use the molds a mixture known as compo was and still is used. Compo was composed of whiting, resin, animal glue, linseed oil and some cellulose, which is used as a binder. When mixed and heated, the mixture resembles putty. To use the mold, a gob of compo was placed on top of the mold and a flat board was placed on top of the gob. The mold was wiped with kerosene to prevent it from sticking. The entire unit was then placed in a press and the excess was pressed out. When the board was removed, the impression remained, which was then sliced off and applied to the frame. Every section on a ornate frame was applied exactly in this manner and even today this is the way it is done. There are a few companies such as Vilas-Mages of Chicago which still produce a modified finished corner frame.

Around 1831, the French painter Louis Daguerre developed a photographic process known as the daguerrotype. The process involved an exposure on a sensitized surface of ruby glass and by chemical means a photograph was made.

Then in approximately 1850, a photographic image was produced on a metal plate. Eventually the ferrotype was created. This process involved coating a lacquered surface that has been coated with collodion, with a silver nitrate preparation. This was later to be known as the tin type because the surface used was a tin plate. No negative was produced in this

Figure 6

Circa 1890
size 16 by 20
Five frame design, gold cylinder compo, cream flat area, typical portrait frame, **very** large wide frame.

Figure 7

Circa 1878
size 10 by 12
Four frame design silver toned in black, cylinder compo design, red velvet liner and inner bead liner, wide frame.

Figure 8

Circa 1885
size 20 by 24
Four frame design, gold leaf design, open network hand cut after compo is applied, very ornate, a Cadillac of frames made yesterday.

Figure 9

Circa 1878
size 10 by 12
Four frame design, silver done in a pewter finish, cylinder mold compo, red velvet liner, inner bead design liner.

process. The entire image was in reverse and if one held a sign up while the picture was being taken, it would read backwards.

The early photos were housed in small brass frames, (Figure 39). They were extremely ornate in nature. Sometimes the outer case that contained the brass frame was impressed with a cameo profile or it might contain a patriotic saying. The case sizes varied but the majority were 2½ by 2¾ inches and were mainly manufactured around 1852. The larger 2½ by 3½ inch size were manufactured later. These cases were very handy and could be carried by purse or placed on top of a table or mantle piece. A case of Gutta Perch was also to appear. These cases were very fine. The material simulated a hard rubber appearance. They were cast and had little brass hinges, (Figure 39). Most of these began to disappear after the Civil War when the photographic process advanced to new methods. Fredrick Scott Archer, (1813-57), introduced the wet glass plate process which produced a negative and thereby also produced larger pictures. Richard Kenneth, (1815-96), produced a dry plate process in 1878. About 1883 an American inventor George Eastman produced a film consisting of a long paper coated with sensitive emulsion. The invention of the roll film marked an end to the era of early photography, and hence the end of the small brass picture frame used for early photographs. (Figure 39) shows examples of these frames.

Growth continued in America and by the mid 1800's, America emerged as a young nation trying to be self sufficient. The importing of finished goods gradually decreased in proportion to the export of cotton, furs, tobacco, lumber and other goods. The country's crude industries were expanding, sometimes by leaps and bounds as new inventions were being placed in use.

Eventually the expanded use of a cylindrical mold opened another avenue of increased production. Then with the old American know-how, stock moulding could be produced by the thousands of feet. The cylinder mold rolled the pressed compo on to the wood stock, and in effect acting like a cookie cutter, it left a compo design on the moulding.

It was found, that the speed at which this operation would run would depend on the sharpness of the mold. If the design was sharp and deep, then it released slowly from the mold, while if the mold was shallow the imprint was faster, So again, with labor costs in mind, fine detailed moulding decreased as production increased. Hence, a sharper design usually indicated an earlier frame.

Time meant money, and applied compo took one to two days to dry. Because compo was used, the cost of this process had a bearing on the final cost of the framing material. Finally it was found that one could "press" a design on the moulding to a limited extent. This was done with a heated die that would burn and impress a design on the moulding, thereby eliminating some of the compo work. A combination of compo and pressed design appeared. Eventually under the guise of "improvement", the pressed design took over. In reality one was getting less for his money. The term, "new and improved", words which are frequently used today, really means "we have eliminated something".

It really took the Civil War to speed mass production techniques. This occurs after every major war. Large wide frames were created by combining various mouldings. This opened up avenues for many different styles. The most prevalent frame was a frame used by artists who traveled from farm to farm and sketched a portrait in charcoal, the "photograph" of yesterday, (Figure 6). The frame was a composite of four frames. The composition was generally oak and compo stock. Up to about 1900 the charcoal sketch was the portrait picture of that era. In this process the 16 x 20 inch frame was the most commonly used. This size is the predominant size of the Victorian era.

Figure 10

Circa 1875
size 22 by 27
Outer frame gold leaf, middle, part carved design, inner liner gold leaf, style similar to 1630 Italian three piece frame.

Inner Frame Figure 11

Circa 1860
size 14 by 17
Multilayer hand carved wood frame, composed of many sheets of thin wood. Each layer carved, very similar to early 16th century Dutch framing.

Figure 12

Circa 1875
size 8 by 10
Walnut cross frame, carved corner embelishments, burnished gold inner liner, typical Americana.

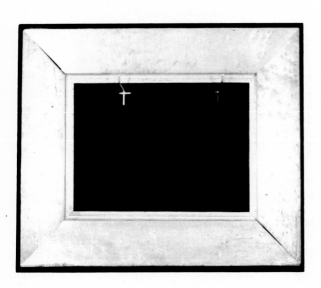

Figure 13

Circa 1740
size 9 by 13
Birds eye maple veneer, English origin, gold leaf liner, cross braced corners.

IV – Early Influences of Frame Distribution

Picture frames and pictures were few and far between in the early Colonial times. The Puritanical simplicity of house decor was prevalent and it was reflected in the clothing, the furniture and the interior of the rooms. The clothing was made of crude hand loom fabrics. There was little embellishment on the clothing, simply because any type of ornamentation would have to be imported. Lace was at a minimum and it was restricted to the neck and cuffs. The furniture had straight lines and turnings were at a minimum. It was designed mainly for use in the home and served no other purpose. A chair was made to be sat upon and nothing else. The rooms were plain and simple, with no wallpaper or even paint. Instead, the walls were natural wood planking or even logs. There was also some plastering which remained white. During these times, to have fancy clothes or fancy pictures on the wall was a show of wealth and was frowned upon and scorned.

As America grew and imports from Europe increased, the trend began to change. Paris was the center of fashions and with the characteristic elegance of the French taste, the clothes began to take on a more elaborate fashion. The French influence was apparent in the furniture with its characteristic curved line features. This was reflected also in the picture frames. More detail began to show on the frame mouldings. Fortunes were being made in America and the desire of many to exhibit their wealth brought the fine frames and paintings from Europe. The masses wanted to copy Europe and this spurred further importing and later imitating the fine frames from the old country.

Nothing spurs on the production of a commodity more than creating a need for it. The picture frame was basically used for paintings, prints and portraits. The gradual expansion of printing facilities helped the producing of engraved pictures. Magazines began to emerge with engravings that were suitable for framing. There was Leslie's Magazine, Peterson's Magazine and the Godey's Lady's Book. Charles Jacobs Peterson founded the Peterson's Magazine in 1842. It was a monthly periodical of women's fashions and literature and was published in Philadelphia. Peterson remained as editor until the magazine merged with another publication and became known as the Ladies National Magazine.

The Godey's Lady's Book was a monthly periodical for women. It was first printed in 1830 by Louis A. Godey. The book contained many fine engravings that were the works of many excellent engravers of the day, as well as many magnificent color plates of fashions. The periodical came out monthly and each publication had a colored fashion plate for that month. These color plates were actually hand-colored with watercolor. Imagine that! To do this, rows of women would be seated at a long table. Each woman would put a certain color on the plate and then pass it to the next person who painted in the next color. This was the process for creating a colored print in that time and obviously involved quite a bit of hand labor. The magazines were also bound together in book form including the twelve copies of each year.

Many of the plates were then framed. The Currier and Ives prints were early lithograph prints that were to have a dominant effect on the growing demand of pictures for hanging. The Currier and Ives prints were distributed by the "tinkers," wagon peddlers who sold tin goods and other items. They penetrated every corner of the countryside. Once people bought these prints, they usually wanted to frame them, and a demand was created for framing material. Stores which handled soap exchanged pictures for soap coupons, and the magazines gave away pictures for subscriptions of the magazine. The Sears and Roebuck catalogues also featured complete framed pictures which sold for around $1.85.

Figure 14

Circa 1860
size 20 by 24
Deep style, simulated grain edge, marbelized inner section, burnished gold lip, outer side finished black.

Inner frame figure 15

Circa 1885
size 8 by 10
Four frame construction, ribbed inset in oak outer frame, black inner frame with carving, speckled liner with inner liner of beaded design.

Figure 16

Circa 1880
size oval 18 by 22
European stick molding, deep, five inches wide, gold leaf finish, wood oval mat leafed in gold.

Figure 17

Circa 1898
size 16 by 20
Three frame design, natural oak outer frame with inset beading, dimensional oak inner frame, gold compo liner.

Inner frame figure 18

Circa 1888
size 3 by 4
Gold leaf compo, walnut toned oak. Compo liner of gold leaf.

Figure 19

Circa 1840
size 8½ by 10½
European frame, gold leaf, multiuse of mold compo, superb design and use of compo trim.

Perhaps one of the most influential developments that was to come was the invention of the lithographic process for multicolor prints. It was this invention which really accelerated the demand for pictures and hence the demand for frames. The process was invented by the Bavarian dramatist Alloys Senefelder (1771-1834) in 1798. He was a native of Prague and as a playwright, he sought a cheap way of printing plays and music. He found that he could print copies by drawing the material out with a greasy crayon on a flat piece of limestone and then inking it, because the ink would only adhere to the greased crayon area. Wetting the surface helped the process because the ink would not adhere to the wet surface that remained. The limestone that was used was 2 to 4 inches in thickness. In time, this process developed into the flat plate process in which the surface was alternately dampened with gum arabic, water, and dilute acid and the ink was rolled onto it. A sheet of paper was then applied and a print was made. When a certain color was desired, a separate stone was made with only the colored area crayoned in. The ink of the desired color was then applied and transferred on the original print, thereby coloring that specific area. For each additional color, a new stone was made. The result was one of the first mass produced color prints. In time, limestone measuring 5 to 7 inches thick and 40 by 60 inches in area were used.

A profusion of prints were to come also from Europe although the paper differed somewhat from ours and the Europeans had a greater variety of textures to draw upon. One limitation was the number of prints that the stones could produce. Eventually this stimulated the development of lithography whereby a metal sheet could be curved into a cylindrical form. This greatly speeded up the printing process.

During the 1800's and particularly the latter part of the century, one was to see a massive barrage of religious scenes and portraits, and with the aid of lithography, many beautiful religious pictures and scenes were created. There was seldom a house that did not have at least one picture of that type. The religious subject matter was the second most commonly used subject for framing, with the charcoal portraits being the first. Today the religious pictures are not wanted. It apparently is not the "vogue" to hang them up and now they are being discarded. I believe that this vogue will change and there will come a day when they will be again in demand. The only trouble is that so many pictures will have been destroyed. They represent a work of art as each creation does. Why destroy something because it does not happen to be in fashion? Art is to be appreciated forever and not for just the next ten years. To create a religious picture, you had to paint love, humility, beauty, and kindness in the faces you portray. Please tell me what is wrong with that?

V — Frame Sizes

Frame size is most important because if the frame is not the right size, then it will not be used. Yesterday's frame sizes did differ from those in common use today. In early Post-Revolutionary times there was no resemblance of any standard size whatsoever. Most primitive frames are varied as to size. It was not until the late 1800's that there began a pattern of standard sizes. The size of 8 x 10 remains common today, but the sizes smaller than 8 x 10 are very rare. The size 10 x 12 was fairly common, but seems to have been replaced by the 9 x 12 size. The most common size for photography today is 11 x 14, but this was not so in earlier times. Most Currier and Ives prints were mounted in 10 x14 frames. A popular size of 14 x 18 exists today but it is virtually impossible to find an early frame of that size. The common size which is close to that dimension is the 14 x 17

Figure 20

Outer frame Circa 1880
size 20 by 28
Black and gold leaf, open network cylinder
compo, delicate application.

Figure 21

Circa 1860
size 8 by 10
Burnished gold, simulated walnut with
carving, gold lip.

Figure 22

Circa 1875
size 22 by 26
Five frame, design, compo applied by mold,
gold leaf.

Inner frame Figure 23

Circa 1881
size 8 by 10
Silver leaf, cylinder compo convex type
frame.

Figure 24

Circa 1885
size 14 by 17
Barbizon type compo, gold leaf, separate
liner gold leaf.

Figure 25

Circa 1885
size 12 by 16
Shaded oak with outer beading, inner liner-
swirl pattern with fluted lip liner, gold leaf.

frame. You may be able to fit the picture but you will have to probably cut into the liner of the frame to allow the painting to fit. The other alternative is to trim the picture.

The most common size used was the 16 x 20 frame, which is still being used today. It was the common general print size and the common portrait size of the late 1800's. The 24 x 30 is another popular size, close to the earlier size of 25 x 30. By 1890 however, the size of 24 x 30 began to appear. One common size today is the standard 24 x 36, and yet years ago it was the 24 x 32 size.

The modern 24 x 48 is a non-existent size in old frames. The size is designed for today's sofas, but it would have been too long for the sofa of yesterday. However, there did exist a size of 18 x 40 that was used for the hallway mirror and for a picture over the sofa. The only sizes that remained steady were the 8 x 10, 12 x 16, 16 x 20, 20 x 24, and 22 x 28.

Perhaps now you will know why you may have been running into difficulty finding a certain size in an old frame. The only way that you can get a certain size is to either compensate with an additional liner or recut a larger frame. Some of the antique sizes that have disappeared with time are the 3½ x 5, 14 x 17, 16 x 24, 22 x 27, 24 x 32, and the 24 x 34.

In regards to cutting an antique frame, some people will feel that a frame should not be cut because its value will be decreased. Unlike most antiques for which this generally holds true, the frame cannot be used unless it fits the item. Unlike most antiques, the frame does not have any use by itself, but is only a component of an entire unit which is basically the picture unit. One can have a million frames, but if a 14 x 15½ inch frame is needed to fit a certain picture, the only way to get it framed with an old frame is to cut a 14 x 17 frame.

The sizes less than 8 x 10 are the rarest. While today we have sizes of 4 x 6, 5 x 7, and 6 x 8, these were almost non-existent yesterday. The reason was simple. There was no demand for these and therefore they for the most part were not made in any quantity. The size patterns for photographs varied considerably because no standard size was determined. The early tin-type picture sizes were 2 x 2½, and 2¾ x 3¼ inches. When a further development of photography took place, the postcard size of 3 x 5½ came into view. After that, a great variety of sizes came into use including 3½ x 5½, 3½ x 5, 4 x 5, and many others. Most of the photographs were destined to be placed in albums. Even today new sizes are becoming popular such as the 3½ x 3½ and many others. Do not expect to find an antique frame of this size. The following chart may help you in determining sizes.

Size Comparison

Yesterday's Sizes	Today's Comparative Size
8 x 10	8 x 10
10 x 12	9 x 12, 10 x 12
10 x 14	10 x 14, 11 x 14
14 x 17	14 x 18
16 x 20	16 x 20
22 x 27	22 x 28
25 x 30	24 x 30
24 x 32	24 x 36
none	24 x 48

One of the reasons you may be having difficulty in locating a frame for a foreign painting is because the European pictures are measured in centimeters and not in inches. Therefore, what may have been a standard measure size in Europe, may not be so here in America. An example of this is the foreign measure 8½ x 10½ inches but our closest standard size is 8 x 10 inches.

Figure 26

Circa 1878
size 20 by 24
Stripped wood frame, very wide, four frame design ideal for primitives, toned wood finish.

Figure 27

Circa 1860
size 19 by 23
European frame thin compo mold design, acorn and oak design, compo corners, gold leaf and gilt combination burnished tips on leaves.

Figure 28

Circa 1880
size 12 by 16
Early compo inlaid in oak frame, wood finished natural, compo wood blended for color.

Figure 29

Circa 1890
size 16 by 20
Portrait frame, four frame design, open network inset Ribbed outer edge and inner liner, petal liner.

VI – Early Prices and Comparison

In the 1898 Sears and Roebuck catalogue, there is an oval mirror frame (Figure 71) that is four inches wide, with an open network design. It contained a French beveled plate mirror. This frame sold for four dollars and eighty-five cents. Today, a plastic reproduction of the same frame with a plate mirror, but without a beveled surface now sells for $150.00.

The first conclusion is that the mirror for $4.85 in 1898 was really a buy! But, was it really? Let us put it in the right perspective. At the time that the frame sold for $4.85, the railroad worker who was generally recognized as the average worker, was making thirty dollars a month. In reality, when you paid the $4.85 for that frame, you really were paying two-thirds of a week's salary. By putting it into the right perspective and comparing the $150.00 cost today with the average wage of $175.00 per week, the cost in comparison is pretty close to being the same.

One must always compare yesterday's prices in this way and not by the sum alone. Many times I would buy old frames with notations on the back such as 85¢, $1.50, etc., and many of these prices were the original prices of the frames. Sometimes the antique dealer, by not realizing this, sold many a frame to me at that price, thinking that perhaps he or she had already priced it as such.

The fact is that basically prices are cheaper today than yesterday because of the advance of technology. However, quality and baroqueness still command a higher price today just as they have in the past. The awareness of cost becomes increasingly apparent as frame design is followed through the years. Although cost has always been noted, the labor part of a commodity was considered to be a minor part years ago, with more emphasis on distribution cost, transportation costs, and raw material cost. As labor began to assert itself, this became a growing cost factor to the manufacturer. In his endeavor to keep the cost down and his profit up, he began to cut his product and eliminate from it extra costs. He was, of course, "improving" his product.

One has to use comparison in order to evaluate antique frames that may not be priced. Let us take a portrait frame, size 16 x 20, made with oak and gold, with a four-frame unit construction, as an example: There is about seven feet of material in each frame unit. At a price of even two dollars a foot for a comparative moulding today each frame unit would cost $14.00. Since there are four parts, then the comparative cost of the frame today is a minimum of $56.00; adding to this its antique value you can closely determine total value. This is, of course, based on a frame in near perfect condition.

Frames with tortoise shell work, carving and other details involving considerable handwork have to be evaluated and one can well see why these frames are valued so highly today.

Walnut frames of the deep variety simply are not made today and never will be. This wood is becoming one of the most valuable woods because of its threatened extinction. Although you should price this frame by its possible replacement value, this will be an increasingly difficult task.

Many of the gold leaf liners are of burnished gold and may even be impressed with a design. No one makes these today and they should be valued at least four to six dollars a running foot.

Frame material with heavy compo work on it can also be valued by comparison. Today a modified European compo moulding with limited trim sells for about six to eight dollars a running foot for material that is about four inches wide. Some early frames were seven to eight inches in width and comparatively would be worth twenty dollars a foot today.

Figure 30

Circa 1878
size 10 by 12
Two frame construction, silver leaf, mold
compo.

Figure 31

Circa 1885
size 8 by 10
Walnut outer frame, inner liner tortoise
speckled finish, gold leaf lip liner.

Figure 32

Circa 1898
size 8 by 14
Oak veneer base, black finish, mold compo
applied, open network corners.

Figure 33

Circa 1890
size 8 by 10
Three frame design, walnut outer frame,
tortoise speckled inner liner, beaded lip
liner of gold.

Figure 34

Circa 1885
size 8 by 10
Four frame design, outer frame feather
laid tortoise shell, basic black and amber,
corners carved design, speckled inner liner,
burnished lip liners.

VII — The Cutting and Assembly of Frames

For each frame made there has to be four pieces of wood with identical angles of forty-five degrees cut at each end. These angles have to be absolutely correct. If there is a deviation of just one degree, there will be a four degree variation by the time that the last corner is assembled. You have to be very accurate. Early frames were cut by hand, using saws that required constant sharpening. Most of the early frames did not have fine mitered corners because of the crudeness of the equipment involved. Sometimes in order to assist in the fastening of large frames, a cross key was cut into the joint to assure a strong tie. The cross key was later discontinued because of the extra work involved.

The compo on the frames made the cutting of them very difficult. Its texture was like sand and the blades that were used to cut it lasted only a few hours before resharpening was required. Today we have hardened steel blades that can last much longer. The carbide tipped blades of today can last three weeks in production before being resharpened.

Cutting old compo frames can prove to be difficult. There are times when you cut into a frame only to have it spring apart. This is because of tension built into the frame through the years, which apparently remains balanced in the frame until it is cut. Old compo becomes like a rock and it can easily break up. Therefore, a bench saw is not recommended to cut old compo frames. It is found that a band saw using hardened steel cutting blades can do a saitsfactory job in cutting.

Today, much of the moulding is cut by a machine known as a chopper. This machine has two very sharp blades set at ninety degrees from each other and with one swipe of the machine, mitered corners are cut into the stick moudling with two opposite forty-five degree angles. It has an action like a guillotine. It is not recommended to cut compo moulding with this cutter because it would quickly dull the blades. Some mouldings cannot be cut on this machine because of their contours, and in those cases, the bench saw must be used.

VIII — Nails of Old

In the early days nails were considered to be a luxury, since each nail had to be hand made. The nails used to nail Christ to the cross were hand made. Blacksmiths were assigned the job of nail-making and whenever they had some free time they spent it making nail after nail. If there was plenty of time, quite a few nails would be made. The village blacksmith also made the iron for the nails at times.

Because of the expense of nails, there was a widespread use of wooden pegs instead of nails in home construction and early furniture. These wooden pegs can be seen today in reconstructed old homes dating back to the 1700's.

Early nails took the form of extremely long metal triangles with a flat head on them. The horseshoe nail of today is similar to the old nail. The iron was crude with much impurity and had little flexibility to it. If you bent the nail, it would simply snap off. It was not until later when steel refining came into its own, that a better grade of steel was used. Eventually a method of stamping out nails of soft iron was found and nail production increased.

Frames used the early stamped nail up to about 1875, when the wire stamped finish nail began to appear. Frames then used a combination of both types of nails. A frame that had all iron nails of the old design usually was dated prior to 1885. An occasional frame may have the old nails in it and be dated 1915, but this is probably because some shop had

Figure 35

Circa 1889
size 16 by 28
Three frame design, open network outer
design, combination cylinder and mold
compo, gold leaf and natural oak.

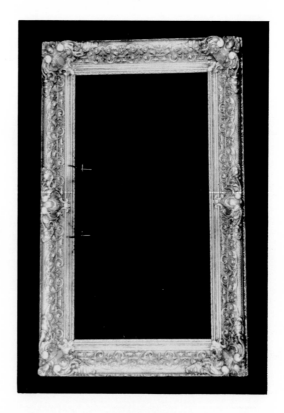

Figure 36

Circa 1885
size 12 by 24
Typical Barbizon style, delicate filigree
design, gold leaf, outer edge and inner edge
beaded style.

Figure 37

Circa 1890
size 12 by 24
Triple frame design, contoured frame, mold
applied compo, whiting surface, tiffany finish (beige tone), gold leaf and gilt finish.

a good supply of the old nails and it took some time to use them up.

Incidentally, the old nails are much in demand and their use on simulating "old antique" furniture has been noted in my travels. It is quite surprising to see so many so-called antiques which are not really antiques. At one time I was offered a fine old chest of drawers dating back, according to the dealer, to the early 1800's. Included in the chest of drawers were fine drawer bottoms of plywood. Another example was a cupboard of rustic construction which the dealer swore was from the 1840 period, yet all along the backing I could detect the faint printing of "SUN-KIST" on it.

You will note that generally little effort was made to hide the nail heads. Some were countersunk, but by far the majority of nails with large heads could be seen. One might imagine that because of the hand labor involved in making frames years ago, the work would be perfect, but no one could be farther from the truth. Most of the frames that I have restored were really inaccurate and crude finishing on corners was predominant. This is due in part to the hand cutting of miters in the frame.

Today, nailing is still used for frames but all the nails are countersunk. There is a type of fastener used today in the production of frames, which has a metal shaft whose profile is shaped like the letter I. It is driven into a precut slot along the miter of the frame and when it is forced in, it has a tendency to pull the frame parts even tighter. Whenever you see this type of fastener you can be sure that the frame is of the most recent vintage.

IX — Glass of Old

Glass has been in existence probably since the earth was first formed. The basic components of glass are silica, better known as sand, and potash or limestone. When these two compounds are subjected to great heat, the alkali acts as a flux and causes the fusion of the material. It is a chemical process in which the silica which has the peculiar property at very high temperatures of acting like a powerful acid, drives out the carbonic acid in the alkali carbonate of soda. The resulting fusion produces glass. This fusion could have taken place in nature under some unique condition of great heat with a mixture of the two compounds that could be found naturally.

There was a time when glass was valued as a monetary item. The Romans developed a glass that contained lead salts, which was to be known as crystal glass. They even developed molds for this glass and introduced the cutting and the decorating of various glass objects. During the era of the Byzantine Empire, the fabrication of glass continued, but by the time the Empire disintegrated in the fifth century, the glass houses had disappeared and the remaining factories had retreated into the forest where production of green, or bottle glass continued.

The earliest sheet glass was made by pouring the molten glass onto a flat surface and spreading it out to form a sheet. This glass had a tendency to have a ring-like formation during the process of hardening. It became known as "bull's-eye glass." The thickness of this glass and others made like it varied, sometimes from 1/16 to 3/16 of an inch. The brush marks would be evident and there were many imperfections. The bubbles in the glass were usually round. There was a difficulty in cutting this glass because of the varied thickness and the stresses formed within the glass. The melting pots for glass were made from powdered clay of the finest type. These pots were produced to hold very large proportions. As late as 1886 Aterbarry & Company of Pittsburgh, who were manufacturers of tableware, were using open melting pots that held 500

Figure 38

Assorted wood compo molds, four outer molds are wood
carved out of maple, center mold is made from asphalt-
sulphur compound impressed with item to be molded.

Figure 39

Various tintypes of the 1852 period.
Left case gutta percha with tintype, center, unusual dual
octagon case with tintypes, right, usual common case
made of cardboard covered with fabric embossed with
designs, velvet interior also embossed with design.

Figure 40

Circa 1910
Triangle mirror
Triple hook mirror made with common
frame stock of that period, simulated
mahogany finish.

to 3500 pounds of molten glass. Around 1890, tank furnaces came into use.

Sheet glass was a cherished possession and it was a fortunate cabin in the pioneer days that had one window containing glass. Incidentally, a substitute for window glass was isin glass which was a crystalline mineral that could be peeled into thin semi-transparent sheets of small dimension.

In 1819, the proprietors of the Pittsburgh Glass Works advertised that they could deliver sheet glass from 7 x 9 to 8 x 24 inches in dimension, packed in boxes containing 100 square feet.

Another method of making glass also came into being. This process consisted of blowing a long cylindrical bubble to about 15 inches in diameter, slicing off the ends, slitting the remaining bubble and allowing it to flatten out. This was a tremendous improvement and this process spurred on the production of sheet glass. In this way larger sheets were manufactured. This glass became known as cylinder glass and there was always a slight curvature to it. The imperfections and bubbles that were present were elongated. There was probably a decrease in the number of imperfections in the sheet as the technique developed. The early cylinder glass was hand blown, but machinery was eventually developed to mechanize the process.

The glass from the mid 1800's and later used only the cylinder glass process. I have found it very nice to use the old glass for old authentic items of antiquity in old frames. It adds something to the entire package.

The color in glass is the result of mineral salts that may have been in the sand or were added to the mixture for a specific color. Iron salts give the characteristic green color that has been widely used in bottles and other vessels. If there is a blue color, then cobalt salts have been added. The greater the quantity of salt used, the more intense is the color. The early daguerrotypes were produced on a ruby-colored glass. This color was produced in the glass by using gold salts.

Some glass will actually fade with time and crystallize to a point that when you try to cut it, the glass will break where you don't want it to.

The sheet glass used today is now made by drawing off the molten glass with a long steel bar of a specific thickness, called a "bait." The thickness of the bar determines the eventual glass thickness. The horizontal bar is raised up, drawing a sheet of molten glass. Controlled cooling solidifies the sheet, which is then bedded on a series of asbestos rollers and eventually cooled and cut to size.

Plate glass involves a different process. Window glass cannot be made uniform because of the way it is made. The variations in thickness creates many problems and causes distortion. This is not objectionable in windows, but in the case of mirrors and optical instruments it can be a problem. Plate glass is made by rolling the glass. The old method involved pouring out molten glass on a table and rolling the material out with a roller. Today the glass is pressed out between two temperature controlled rollers and a sheet of glass is created that could be as much as one inch in thickness. The glass temperature must be accurately controlled in order to anneal the glass properly. The plate glass is cut and placed on a uniform surface and, with the use of emery, sand or other grinding materials, the surface is ground to a uniform specification. The final step is polishing the plate glass with rouge. There are perhaps ten to twelve different stages to the grinding and polishing. Improvements in the process have been made and now both sides of the plate glass can be polished at the same time.

Non-glare glass is widely being used today because the glare factor is considerably lessened. The cost of this glass has come down in recent years and has proven to be more desirable by the public than regular glass. For a direct application to pastels or pictures it has proven to be useful. The only time when I would not recommend non-glare glass would

Left Figure 41

Circa 1890
size 16 by 20
Three frame construction Gold leaf.
Oval opening.

Right Figure 42

Circa 1885
size 16 by 20
Four frame construction gold leaf
liners with gilt finish parts, came
also with ivory and gilt finish.

Left Figure 43

Circa 1885
size 8 by 10
Compo mold applied, modified oval,
base four part wood construction,
gold leaf.

Right Figure 44

Circa 1885
size 8 by 10
Oval wood with applied whiting by
template, compo by mold, gold leaf,
also simulated walnut.

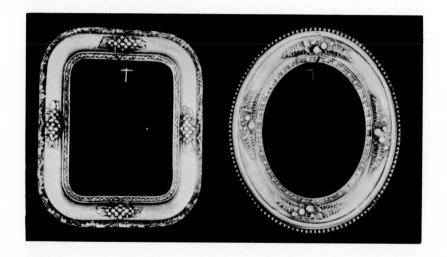

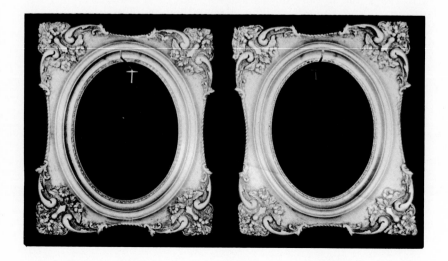

Figure 45

Circa 1850
size approx 8 by 10
Gold leaf, probably European Hand
contoured formed oval with applied compo trim. Matched pair.

be if the glass is to be installed more than 1/16 of an inch away. Because of the nature of the glass the picture begins to fade away when the installation is further than 1/16 of an inch or so. If the item is a fan or some object in a deep shadow box then you would have to use regular glass to see it.

Some people feel that they would rather not use glass at all. Unless the item is completely sealed, like an oil painting, or something else impervious to the elements, it is an unwise procedure to do without glass. Paper mats and items of cloth etc., that are exposed to air will get flabby and buckle. The items will also soil easily, and grease and cigarette smoke will cover the picture.

X — The Back of the Old Picture Frames

It is interesting to see what secrets the back of an old picture frame will relate to us. There is an old belief that one will, on occasion, find money, perhaps even a considerable amount, hidden in the back of an old picture frame. It would seem logical to hide money there, just as logical as under a mattress, or perhaps under a drawer. Perhaps some of the antique dealers may have found some money, but I can attest that of the ten thousand frames that I have personally opened, I have yet to find one dollar. There was a time that I did find a love letter, from a sixteen-year-old girl to some boy.

There are some rewards, however. One time while opening up an old frame I found a beautiful rare Currier and Ives print that was behind another picture in the frame. This print turned out to be a rare one and it was like finding a hundred dollar bill in a frame.

The finest finds which I have discovered behind frames were the newspapers. The papers contained their dates and it was in this way that I was eventually able to determine the approximate period of the various frames. By observing the date and the design I was able by repetition, and analysis, to determine when a certain frame design appeared and when it finally disappeared. The newspapers also contained many interesting news stories and while there were many articles attesting to the latest cancer cures, there were also many testimonials of dropsy and nerve disorder cures.

For the backing materials of frames a thin piece of wood was used. First, the print or item was placed on heavy cardboard, then another cardboard sheet covered the latter, and thin pieces of wood approximately $\frac{1}{8}$ inch thick formed the final backing. This process apparently endured sucessfully as it protected the print even today. The backing material, however, was affected by moisture, because it was seldom sealed by paper, and when it was, the paper life was limited to 30-40 years. The paper was important because it was a barrier to moisture. It also unfortunately held moisture. Moisture is a detriment to pictures in frames. It will act upon the paper and if there is any free sulfurous acid in the paper stock the print will form spots, stains and marks. There is nothing that can be done to eliminate the stains. They are caused by a chemical change and cannot be reversed. Many early prints, engravings and lithographs are plagued by these stains, which are aggravated by moisture.

Today illustration board is used as backing as effectively as cardboard. In the case of cardboard it is recommended that a cover sheet of a good grade of white paper be used to cover the back of the picture prior to covering with cardboard. Cardboard is acidic in nature and will in time stain the picture unless a white sheet separates it. Illustration board is covered with white paper which is chemically neutral. If this were not true the board would yellow and darken because of the moisture in the air. Newsprint will yellow because it is composed of acidic wood pulp.

Some of the frames of the 1800's will contain old charcoal drawings

Figure 46

Circa 1890
size 16 by 20
Laminated oak ply with molded compo trim.
frame contoured with oval opening,
gilt finish.

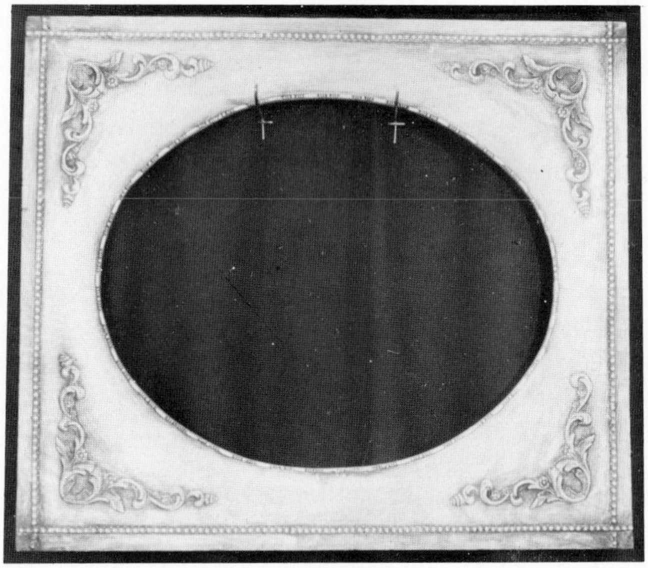

Figure 47

Circa 1895
size 16 by 20
Laminated oak base with applied molded
compo trim, gilt finish.

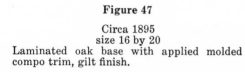

Figure 48

Circa 1875
size 20 by 24
Magnificent example of compo work, four
frame construction, gold leaf finish.

which were the "photographs" of that period. Many of these drawings were finely done and many people assume that these drawings are actually photographs. During this period there were many roving artists occupied in this profession of sketching people for portraits. I would say that perhaps eighty per cent of all pictures found in 16 x 20 frames were either charcoal sketches of people, lithograph prints or certificates of weddings, baptism and graduations. Some frames were used to house the casket picture of the individual, probably because there was no other picture of record of the person. It was also a common practice to frame the casket name plate.

Among the most fascinating items found are woven hair bracelets and woven hair floral designs. These were intricately made by weaving human hair into designs that were sometimes very elaborate.

Some of the mats that were used in early days represent some very fine works of art. There would be intricately cut out sections with colored paper showing through the various sections of the mat (figure C/8). It was obvious that considerable time was spent in the creation of a mat.

The material used to hang the picture varied. Besides the screw eyes we use today, there would also be nails and screws used with wire that was made of copper or brass. Sometimes a cord was used to hang the picture from a moulding that was placed about eighteen inches from the ceiling. The cord was usually red and had a tassle center piece as ornamentation. Ceilings were at least ten feet high in the 1800's so this method of hanging was feasible. As the ceiling became lower this practice disappeared.

XI – Ovals

Oval frames are of great interest because of their odd shape. There seems to be an attraction about this elongated circle. The oval is really a combination of two circles that have a specified ratio distance between their centers. One cannot simply whip up an oval for a certain size easily without having a jig made to create this odd size. There is practically no one that will custom make an oval for you unless you are interested in a thousand of them.

In order to make the old oval, sections of wood were dovetailed and joined together. The joined section is then cut to the outer size of the frame and the outer edge is routed away, by means of a shaper. The unit is then placed on a jig setup and the inner lip is shaped out. This is always a dangerous procedure and many a finger has been lost in this operation. Because of the greater amount of work involved, the cost of an oval is greater than that of a conventional frame. The section could be made up of four, six or even eight pieces of wood. After forming the oval, the unit was generally covered with whiting by means of the template that had a profile slightly larger than the oval. Compo trim was then added to the oval.

Back in the early 1800's there began a production of an especially beautiful piece of work. This was the walnut oval (Figure 62). It was usually constructed of four pieces of walnut that were joined and shaped to form the oval. In a time when the only sources of power were water and steam, it is most remarkable to observe the results of their workmanship.

The oval was beautifully finished and hand coated with many coats of shellac which were hand rubbed between each coat to an absolutely smooth finish. Finally a gold leaf liner was added to the inner lip. The liner itself was a thing to behold. It was usually made with joined pieces of wood and then covered with whiting and finished just like frames that were gold leafed. The final leafing on the liner was burnished and

Figure 49

Circa 1890
size 20 inch round
Cylinder compo applied, open network routed out after application, gilt finish.

Left Figure 50

Circa 1860
size 8 by 10
Walnut, four section, Pressed in
brass inner liner.

Right Figure 51

Circa 1880
size 8 by 10
Gold leaf lip, simulated walnut
graining, compo decoration.

Left Figure 52

Circa 1895
size 8 by 10
Basic black finish, gold lip, applied
compo trim and lip.

Right Figure 53

Circa 1895
size 8 by 10
Tortoise speckled finish, applied
compo trim and lip.

fitted to the oval. Productions of these ovals, for the most part, ceased around 1864. Practically all the ovals of this type are over 100 years old.

Toward the end of the production period, the gold leaf liner was replaced by a brass snap-on liner used basically to reduce the cost (Figure 51). The value of these ovals depends upon the liners. If the liner is missing, then the value is decreased, and the condition of a remaining liner is equally important. The wood part of the oval can usually be repaired or even refinished, but the liners need more work to be restored and it is impossible to replace them if they are missing. Since few people know the true story of these ovals, they are for the most part underpriced.

Because the demands were growing for the oval, another approach to manufacturing developed. Four pieces of basswood or other woods were dovetailed and joined. The oval was cut as before on the outer edge, then shaped on the edge and inner lip. The back was oblong routed to receive a picture and glass without having to cut into an oval. The next step was to place the oval in a jig on a potter's wheel. Then through the use of a template and whiting, a smooth surface was formed on the rough oval and the oval was removed and allowed to dry. After a certain period, the oval was ready for a compo application or simulated wood finish.

If the oval was to have a simulated walnut finish, then the finishers took over, creating magnificent duplications of walnut, which was one of America's favorite woods. Sometimes it is so well done that unless it is very closely examined, one cannot tell the difference.

In the early period, there were many variations of wood finishing, both by themselves and with combinations of compo and wood.

By the use of the compo molds, suitable trim was applied to the lip, the rim and the ornaments on the face. You can almost judge the age of the oval by the amount of trim it has. Very early ovals are loaded with compo trim. The gold leaf accent is in profusion and the lip is covered with gold leaf. The molded sections are very sharp in detail (Figure 57).

Pre-civil war ovals that have compo work on them have a certain characteristic of their own. You feel as you look at them that nothing was spared to produce a creation of workmanship. Each piece consisted of an unusual amount of artistic compo work and an ingenuity of assembly, combined with a perfection in the joining of the pieces involved. This was all to change with the passing of time.

The larger types of ovals were generally used for portraits or mirrors. The basic structure differed slightly, but they can be judged on the same basis as the smaller types. They were usually constructed by using eight pieces of wood which were dovetailed together. The finishing of these ovals was the same as that of the smaller ovals. Two of the most common sizes were 14 x 17 and 16 by 20. Some of these were to exhibit an open network design with compo trim. Again, the frame with greater compo trim or greater detail work on the face was generally older.

A companion to the 16 x 20 frame was an 18 x 40 inch oval with a beveled plate mirror (Figure 71). This was the hallway mirror of the late 1800's. Other 18 x 40 frames were to come but the compo trim was being brought to a minimum, or even eliminated completely.

A size of about 13½ x 19½ oval came into use during the late 1800's (Figure 60). It sometimes had a convex or bubble glass as part of its construction. Most of these ovals were about three inches in width and usually were flat in styling with only a slight beveling to the profile of the oval. Eventually the oval was to gradually shrink in width. By the time 1890 came one could see the change occurring in the ovals. The decorative compo face pieces or ornamentation were getting smaller and smaller. The outer trim was the first to go, and the face pieces were next. By 1898 only the lip compo remained and it was being gilted with gold paint. All of this was under the guise of advancement and progress. Finally by 1910 or so, there was really progress — nothing was applied

Figure C-1
Circa 1885, size 16x20
gold leaf, mold compo applied, contoured back.

Figure C-2
Circa 1880, size 8x10
three frame design, outer trim custom formed, oak and silver leaf, silver liner.

Figure C-3
Circa 1870, size 18x22
red velvet, gold leaf, silver leaf, mold compo.

Figure C-4
Circa 1890, size 8x13
green velvet, tiffany with gilt, three frame design.

Figure C-5
Circa 1880 size, 18x22
deep gold leaf, oval inner liner of wood separate and leafed.

Figure C-6
Circa 1875, size 16x20
black with gold leaf mold compo.

Figure C-7
Circa 1885, size 16x20
contoured oval opening gold leaf, applied compo from molds.

Figure C-8
Circa 1875, size 10x14
simulated wood grain burnished gold liner.

Figure C-9
Circa 1840, size 8½x10½
gold leaf, multi use of mold compo, European frame.

Figure C-10
Circa 1885, size 16x20
five frame design, gilt liners and burnished gold liner combinations.

Figure C-11
Circa 1875, size 8x10
oak-compo combination, three frame design, black tortoise, gold compo liner.

Figure C-12
Circa 1895, size 10x12
Biege, gold tipping, three frame Victorian, open network center.

Figure C-13
Circa 1885, size 8x10
four frame construction ribbed inset oak, speckled liner, beaded inner liner.

Figure C-14
Circa 1880, size 6x8
Outer frame basswood, toned, inner liner black with design hand cut into it. Black edge.

Figure C-15
Circa 1860, size 8x10
Amber toned tortoise sheel finish, burnished gold lip and edge, carved corner designs.

Figure C-16
Circa 1860 size 8x10
walnut hand carved cross frame, comes also with gold liners.

Figure C-17
Circa 1880, size 10x12
black edge with carvings burnished gold liner.

Figure C-18
Circa 1870
standing frame, black with carvings beautiful example of mats with intricate design.

Figure C-19
Circa 1880 size 8x10
simulated mahogany with carving, four frame construction, sand coated gold liner.

Figure C-20
Circa 1888, size 3x4
four frame type, style same as portrait types but unusually small and rare, oak and gold leaf on cylinder compo.

Figure C-21
Circa 1865, size 10x14
walnut with design cuts, oval gold leaf liner.

Figure C-22
Circa 1860, size 10x14
Gold leaf, oval inset, deep, probably European mold compo applied corners.

Figure C-23
Circa 1895, size 16x20
toned wood and cylinder compo, four frame type portrait type frame.

Figure C-24
Circa 1865, size 22x27
European style, black, gold leaf on applied mold compo.

Figure C-25
Circa 1885, size 10x14
mold compo applied to oak, silver leaf, wood natural finish.

Figure C-26
Circa 1885 size 8x10
tortoise finish liners, gold liners, outer frame gold finish, typical tortoise shell frames of that era.

Figure C-27
Circa 1880, size 8x10
wide gold leaf with mold compo, silver liner.

Figure C-28
Circa 1880, size 8x10
Tortoise shell finish, burnished gold accents, carved designs in frame and corner.

Figure C-29
Circa 1890. size 4x5
Oak and silver combination, Three frame design, rare small size.

Figure C-30
Circa 1879, size 8x10
example of tortoise shell with blue accent, rare.

to the oval, leaving simply an oval with a painted finish of some type (Figure 55).

The larger ovals were subjected to the same manner. It soon became the vogue to frame a three inch wide, semi-flat oval with a simulated wood finish, perpendicular to the frame grain. The graining was to simulate mahogany which was the fashionable wood of that period. The lip was painted black. By 1915 or so, the frame had shrunk in width to 1½ inches.

Nothing shows the progress of construction and the cost factor more than the ovals. It is an alarming example of how progress continues, mainly by eliminating something. Is that not true also of progress today?

Today the ovals are cut from either plywood or solid pieces of wood, although some European ovals are dovetailed. The oval is rough cut and then shaped out to form an oval. When the first plywood frames came into existence, there was considerable difficulty with the material because of delamination. Some of the frames received wet compo and the water caused this difficulty. The early frames simply fell apart. It was not until the glue was changed to one with better waterproofing characteristics that the problems were solved.

Most of the recent ovals are of simple lines, with no compo trim. Instead, they rely on finishes which can vary from plain colors to delicate multi finishes. The American ovals are usually stained and have a gilt liner or finish, or are painted black with a gilt finish lip. The European frames are more delicate. The German ovals can be stained but they have a metallic lip. The imitation leaf which is used adds a touch of quality to the ovals. The Italian ovals are even finer with decorative accent trim, and are sometimes inlaid with imitation gold leaf. They may be further embellished with hand-painted flowers or whatever one wants. All of this indicates that hand work is involved and the resulting oval can better be appreciated. Europe still produces the fine detail work on frames and picture frame moulding while American frames rely more on output and mass production.

The influx of the plastic ovals is now apparent. It is our answer to mass production of a product. The growing scarcity of wood will have a direct bearing on eventual plastic production of stick moulding.

One objection to the plastic oval, or stick moulding, is that one cannot insert a nail into the material, although there have been strides in that direction. Some types of casting material, such as compressed sawdust mixtures, will take a nail. Ultimately there will be massive duplication of the old, beautiful ovals, using the plastic injection process. This process consists of injecting a foam plastic into a mold, previously prepared by covering a frame with a latex compound which is stripped off after curing. The product can then be finished to look like the original. The cost will be moderately high because of the hand labor involved.

XII — About Mirrors

The first mirror on earth was a pool of water. Prehistoric man was the first to see his image on the reflective surface of water. Eventually other reflective surfaces were to appear. In early biblical times a polished brass mirror was used and bronze mirrors were used by the Romans. The use of a polished metal surface was used throughout the ancient world. The most highly prized mirror was one of polished silver. The first recorded mirrors as we know them today were made around the year 1300, by coating a piece of glass with an amalgam of tin and mercury. The surface was cleaned, then covered over with tin foil which had been rubbed with mercury. With the use of cloths and weights, the surface was pressed for about a day and eventually a beautiful mirror surface was formed.

Mirrors were generally held by hand and it was not until the 16th century that mirrors were hung on walls. The finest mirrors were created by Venetian workmen who received state protection in the manufacture of mirrors. Venice was to become the main supplier of mirrors for the entire world. All of the early mirrors which came to the colonies were of Venetian manufacture. The first mirrors from England came around 1670.

All of the mirrors in early America were imported. The early frames were made of ebony, olivewood and walnut. Most of the mirrors had a headboard design which varied. There would be spirals, intricate cutouts, mantel tops, soffet designs, and sometimes intricate interweaves which centered around the top of the frame. The sides were limited to spiral columns, plain shafts or inlaid wood.

The open flowing lines of the Chippendale style appeared around 1750. In 1812 there appeared a style of mirror that became known as the Empire style of frame (Figure 108). This frame had two columns that were spiraled with one column on each side. The top was built out with a shelf-like effect and had small wooden balls around the bottom of this shelf. The mirror glass itself was small and it usually had a scene of some type painted on the top half of the frame. The scene would be separated from the mirror by a thin piece of wood. During the period of the war of 1812 it was a common practice to depict war scenes or scenes of a patriotic nature on the glass. Later, flowers and landscapes were painted, usually on glass.

Very early mercury mirrors were small because the sheet glass made at that time was limited in size. As the quality of the glass improved, the clarity of the image also improved. Early mirrors were wavy and full of defects. The only way that one could get fine mirror glass was to have a thick piece of glass ground to perfection. This is like the plate glass of today. Machinery had not been developed to produce this type of glass.

The mirror was often framed as a specific item with special embellishments that the average picture frame would not have. The mirror would reflect the furniture of its period and would tie in with the motif of that design. As the technique of making large sheet glass for mirrors improved, the mirrors increased in size. Early mirrors were made in sections so as to increase the illusion of a larger area. This was to continue until about 1840.

Towards the end of the seventeenth century, England was one of the major countries producing mirror stock. Shortly after that France began to produce the famed French mirror stock, and was also known for their beveled mirrors.

A German chemist, Justus Von Liebig, developed a process to back glass with a silver coating. His procedure called for a silver salt to be reduced to pure silver on a glass surface. A reducing salt solution, such as tin chloride, was poured on a glass surface which had been cleaned. A silver nitrate solution was then applied to the surface and allowed to stand. In a short time the silver nitrate was reduced to pure silver on the glass surface. The residue was allowed to dry and then sealed with shellac.

Today the silvering is done by means of a spray. The surface is sprayed with a reducing solution and then with a silver solution. The reduction is almost instantaneous, and afterwards a fixative solution was sprayed on and allowed to dry. The procedure is much quicker than the old steam-table silver nitrate method.

In America there began to appear some specific styles of mirrors. An example of these was a style of mirror that was commonly used in the kitchen and gradually found its way to other rooms (or vice versa). The kitchen was the bathroom of yesterday, where father would shave, wash, etc. This mirror had rounded corners on the bottom with the top rounded out (Figure 63). The mirror was a mercury type and the glass had many

Figure 54

Circa 1920
size 22 by 28
Two inches wide, tiffany finish with gilt
edging, cylinder compo, multi wood section
base.

Figure 55

Circa 1919
size 16 by 20
Simple design, simulated wood grain on
whiting coated surface. Multi wood section
base.

Figure 56

Circa 1895
size 16 by 20
Simple with applied compo pieces, gilt finish.

Figure 57

Circa 1885
size 14 by 17
Impressed design on whiting base, then applied compo from mold, gold leaf finish, with
color added to flower design.

imperfections because of the crudeness in glass manufacture at that time. The surface of the frame was either fluted or had many step designs on it. The frame was either very plain or finished in black or mahogany color. Sometimes it was embellished with compo parts and gold leafed (figure 73). The lip was applied compo and was usually gold leafed. The size would vary from about 8 x 10 to 20 x 34 inches. At the turn of the century the mirror frame gradually disappeared, while other styles that were more acceptable to the mode of the day took over.

Toward the end of the 19th century the mirror in America took many forms. The traditional headboard mirror continued but it was really tied in with period furniture and also appeared in bedroom sets. The hallway mirror began to appear in ovals or long decorative mirrors. The ovals varied in size framing up to about 18 x 40 inch mirrors. The mirrors were sometimes of an open network type (Figure 49) and were finished in gold gilt paint. The long oblong frame was also made with a mirror which measured about 18 x 40 inches (Figure 77). It was also very ornate, sometimes almost eight inches wide and finished in gilt paint. These mirrors were very popular and almost every home had one in the hallway. This was probably due partially to the fact that they were featured in the Sears Roebuck catalogue.

It was also discovered that one could have a mirror by taking a picture frame and putting a mirror glass into it. The traditional approach to mirrors was soon ignored in America, where they had been tied to the furniture of a period design. Suddenly the housewife had no limitations and when she wanted a mirror on the wall she merely took a picture frame and put a mirror glass in it. Many of the antique frames that are sold today are used as mirrors because they are wide and impressive with their ornamentation. Sometimes it is difficult for a housewife to decide what to put in this type of frame, but by using it to frame a mirror she creates an accented piece that can take its place in almost any decor. This occasional piece stands out and forms an interesting focal point.

XIII — Gold and Silver Leafing

Gold, which has the chemical symbol Au, and the atomic weight of 197.2 is a malleable yellowish metal which is not prone to oxidation and resists chemical reaction with other elements. It is estimated that if all the gold ever mined in the world were placed in a room, the dimensions of that room would be fifty-five feet square by fifty-five feet high.

Gold has been an attractive metal since time is first recorded. It is one of the metals that can be found in a pure state on occasions. This was undoubtedly first noticed when some ore containing the metal oozed out pure gold in a molten state under some great heat or in a fire. Early man found the metal to be malleable and it was used by them as ornamentations. As everyone knows the Incas were famous for their creations of gold inlay and castings.

Gold was highly prized because of its use and beauty. This metal has the same attraction today. Anything made of this metal is valuable— people hoard it, worship it, and have even killed for it. The metal is used as a monetary standard and as a medium of international exchange.

The use of gold in framing was inevitable. The shimmering beauty of the metal was so attractive that it was highly desirable to cover frames with it. Applications of gold leaf for decoration and protection can readily be seen on church steeples, temples, interiors of rooms, furniture and even outside walls and fences. The monks used to spend months carefully leafing the main letters of words in their hand-recorded books and bibles. Meticulously the monks hunched over their work and carefully designed

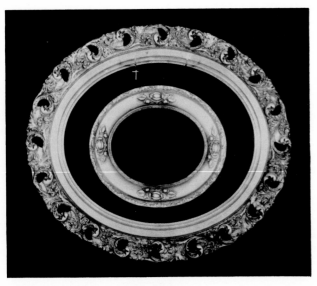

Figure 58

Circa 1890
size 16 by 20
Open network cylinder compo outer rim, inner liner plain, earlier liners embossed, gold color.

Figure 59

inner frame
Circa 1878, size 8 by 10
Gold leaf, compo trim.

Figure 60

Circa 1890
size 14 by 19
Gold, compo trim, combination whiting box finish, with mold compo.

Figure 61

Circa 1890
size 14 by 20
Variation oval, gold finished with compo molded parts.

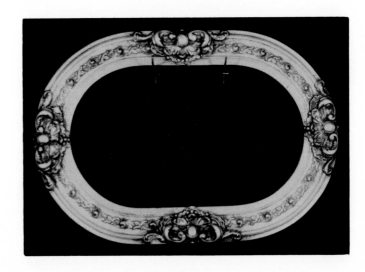

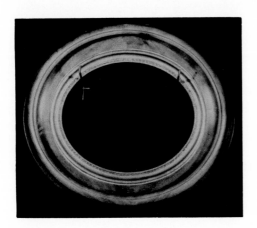

Figure 62

Circa 1850
size 8 by 10
Solid walnut in four sections, gold leaf inner liner.

the letter, applied the sealer, the size, and finally the thin gold leaf.

Gold leaf was made by taking a small nugget of gold and placing it between two pieces of leather, then pounding out the nugget until it became a gradually expanding sheet of gold. The men that did this were known as gold beaters. As the sheet enlarged it was recut until the pounding of the metal resulted in a sheet so thin one could see through it. The leaf was eventually trimmed to about 3½ inches square.

Pure gold is twenty-four karats. All gold leaf has a small amount of impurity, basically silver. Twenty-four karat leaf has a deep color, and the smaller the karat number the lighter the leaf becomes.

An eighteen karat gold leaf is a light lemon gold color. By adding more silver to the gold, sixteen karat gold leaf is produced. Twelve karat gold with a large amount of silver is called white gold, and its leaf has some superior properties. There is less tarnishing and the leaf is more brilliant.

The material that is used to adhere the leaf to the frame is known as gold size. The size is actually a varnish which dries slowly and has a tacky period during drying. There are two basic types of gold size, one is a slow size known as oil size and the other is a faster type of size, or more commonly known as a quick size which comprises a much larger group. The tacky period is considerably shorter and lasts from one to five hours. In leafing a time schedule had to be arranged so that once the size was applied, there would be a specific tack period in which the leaf had to be applied. If the size was left on too long it would dry and would have to be reworked again. This would sometimes ruin an entire lot.

There was also an old sizing called water size. This was a gelatin or glue dissolved in hot water and applied. The surface was then moistened and the gold leaf was applied. Very early gold leaf was done in this manner, but today the basic quick size is the most common one used.

The final result of the leafing always depended on the surface on which it was applied. Gold leaf merely reflects the surface that it was put on. The smoother the surface, the finer the results. On some frames the whiting box was used to apply a uniform coating of whiting on the frame. A template which was slightly larger than the profile was used to smooth the whiting on. The result of that operation was to give a smooth glass-like surface to the frame. The other coating that was applied was red clay. This material was applied and sanded, and the procedure was repeated until a smooth surface resulted. Shellac was next applied, coat after coat until a non-absorbent surface was created. If there was any absorption at all the gold leaf would not adhere because the size would seep into the frame and would not stay on the surface.

After the leaf was applied there came the matter of overlapping the applied leaf with shellac to lay and glue the remaining overlapped gold leaf edges. The process of applying the shellac helped to press down and seal the gold leaf to the intricate designs that were present. A final factor was the toning that shellac gave to the leaf. There was an aging color applied when shellac was used.

A coating of varnish was the final touch of the leafing and the toning could then begin. The main purpose of the final varnish coat was to protect the gold surface during the toning process, because otherwise the rubbing done during the toning would simply rub the gold leaf off. The leaf is so thin that one should never use an abrasive on the surface.

Today virtually all of the "gold leafing" is done by using a composition imitation leaf. The size of the sheet is 5½ x 5½ inches. One way to tell that it has been used on a certain frame is to measure the overlapped joints, which should be approximately the same measure. While imitation leaf does not have all the attributes of actual gold leaf, it is for the most part, more than sufficient for metal leafing today.

The imitation leaf is composed of brass. It is easier to apply than the actual gold leaf, because it is slightly thicker. One drawback is that

Left Figure 63

Circa 1895
size 12 by 20
Typical kitchen shaving mirror
style, tortoise speckled finish, gilt
finished lip.

Right Figure 64

Circa 1905
size 14 by 20
Simulated wood grain, black strip-
ing, black lip. Semi-oval shape.

Figure 65

Circa 1890
Custom size, two frame design, outer oak
and cylinder compo, bead silver liner.

Figure 66

Circa 1910
size 16 by 20
Modified contour frame, mold compo corners, simulated wood grain finish.

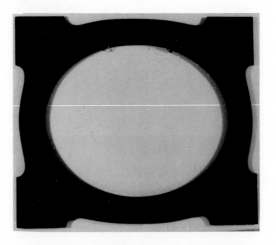

Figure 67

Circa 1900
size 16 by 20
Oak veneer base, oval opening, mold compo
trim, black finish, also came natural oak.

imitation leaf will tarnish unless it is sealed with shellac and other sealers. Gold leaf, on the other hand, does not tarnish readily and only a coat or two of shellac is needed to protect the leaf itself.

Much of the metal leaf today is finished as antique gold, in one way or another. A bright metal finish is not pleasing to look at and it has a brassy new look. Because of the antiquing, it was not necessary to give a good clay or surfacing base on which to apply the leaf. These steps were reduced to a minimum, and the public was conditioned to accept something else.

Most of the base toning of the metal leaf is either French gray, burnt umber, raw umber or dark gray. The method of application is found in the toning section of this book.

Practically all of the "silver" leafing done today is with aluminum leaf. In this case the aluminum leaf is superior to actual silver leaf. If the aluminum leaf had been available in the 19th century it would have cost more than the gold or silver because the extraction process for aluminum had not been developed. The aluminum has a fine sheen and a good body for application. Unlike silver, aluminum does not tarnish, and therefore could maintain a luster for a long time. The aluminum lends itself well as a "pewter" finish which is an aluminum leaf treated with a black glaze to simulate pewter.

The size of the sheets is also 5½ x 5¼ inches. Both composition leaf and the aluminum leaf are now being made in Italy, Germany and Japan.

Cost was still a factor years ago. Because of the greater cost of gold leaf it was found that one could simulate the gold leaf liners by dyeing the silver leaf with an aniline dye. What a surprise it was to clean a "gold" liner only to have it turn to silver. During World War II, when composition leaf was in short supply the process of dyeing aluminum leaf with the same types of dyes produced a simulated gold finish.

You can only do a limited amount of cleaning on a gold leaf surface. Spotting and stains cannot be removed because they are the result of chemical change. The leaf is so thin that to use any abrasive would remove the leaf. Common grease and dirt can be removed by the use of a soap solution or paint thinners. When one uses water it must be done quickly and dried immediately or damage can result.

Silver leaf and Palladium leaf were applied in the same manner as the gold leaf. The silver leaf had to be well sealed because of its tendency to tarnish. The palladium leaf is a silvery leaf that was used extensively as a substitute for silver leaf. It was difficult to work with and was replaced by twelve karat gold leaf.

XIV — The Types of Wood Used

In order to have a picture frame you have to have a wood that will be stable, resist warping, have low shrinkage properties and be able to take the desired finishes. Of all the different types of wood on the market, only certain types have been proven to be value and have the desired properties.

Basswood

Basswood, by far has been the most common wood used in the manufacture of picture frame moulding. The wood is found, to some extent, throughout the eastern part of the United States. The tree can be found in the Great Lakes regions with the greatest concentration around Lake Superior. It is one of the softest of the hardwoods. The color of the

Right Figure 68

Circa 1910
size 24 by 36
Oval odd shaped
Mold applied compo, shaped wood frame
base, copy of 1780 design.

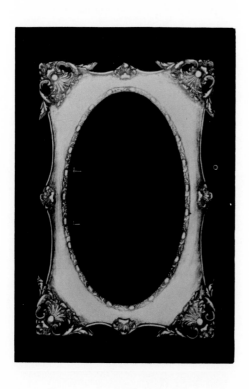

Left Figure 69

Circa 1890
size 14 by 24
Mold compo applied, silver leaf on oak plywood base. Frame contoured.

Right Figure 70

Circa 1895
size 12 by 20
Three frame design, oak outer frame, cylinder compo inner frame, oval embossed
liner mold applied as one piece, gold leaf
finish.

sapwood is almost a grainless white, while the heart tends to lean toward the light brown color. The wood is also used in toymaking, venetian blinds, drawing boards, boxes, furniture sections and many other items that require a stable, clean wood.

Basswood can be readily nailed and can even be worked with without predrilling. There is no splitting tendency as there may be with other woods. Because of the lack of a predominant grain, basswood can be stained easily, but in this field there are other woods that can take a stain better than basswood. Basswood is soft enough to take the hot press designs very well. Many of the fine "pine frames" that some dealers display are not pine at all but basswood. Many dealers are not familiar with the fact that basswood was the most common wood used, and may not recognize the wood when they see it. Pine does have a predominant grain as opposed to the non-grain of basswood. With this knowledge perhaps the dealers can separate the two woods.

Walnut

Walnut was a very desirable wood for cabinets and frames with a natural finish. It is a very valuable wood for furniture and other wood accessories. The wood is not found in great stands but more in isolated groups. The tree grows all over the eastern half of the United States with the greatest concentration in the Ohio valley, the southern Appalachian mountains and Tennessee. A walnut log is seldom over eight feet in length and the width is seldom wider than six inches today. In earlier times the quantity of walnut was greater but it was still a premium wood and there were numerous attempts to duplicate its finish.

The wood has a very high degree of stability and it is one of our best woods for carving. It sands cleanly and takes a natural finish of which there is no equivalent. Most of the color is reddish brown, although the sap wood is much lighter, but by covering the wood with sawdust and then steaming it, the sapwood takes on the same color as the heartwood. The wood has an open grain, but it can be filled without much difficulty. It is usually predrilled for nailing but can take small nails without splitting. Most of the walnut is of the so-called black walnut variety and the wood can be made to look darker by applying stain. Walnut is almost always finished in a natural color.

During the 1800's walnut and oak were the two naturally finished woods that were used. The cheaper basswood and poplar were sometimes stained to look like walnut. Gumwood with a walnut stain creates a good copy of the real thing.

Poplar

Poplar was another wood that was used extensively and it can be considered a hard basswood if a comparison is to be made. The pores are small, and the heartwood has a greenish color, while the sapwood is much lighter. The color approaches a bland white appearance. The wood will take a nail readily, can be glued successfully and can also be worked with hand tools and carved easily. It has better staining properties than basswood, but it can also take the hot press design readily. Some people feel that because it is harder than basswood, the hot design will be much sharper than when cut into basswood.

The concentrations of poplar stands are located in the Ohio Valley section and in the Appalachian Mountain region. The wood is also used for novelties, furniture, boxes, musical instruments, wood veneering, store fixtures and house trim.

Oak

Oak is one of the most common hardwoods in the United States. There

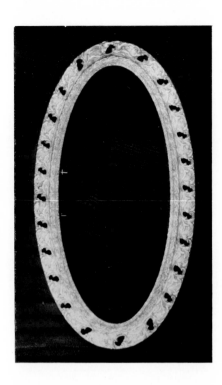

Figure 71

Circa 1895
size 18 by 40
Open network, cylinder compo dual design,
gilt fine frame used commonly as hallway
mirror with beveled mirror. Valuation is
with beveled mirror in good condition.

Figure 72

Circa 1880
size 20 by 30
Gold leaf, embossed inner area, burnished
lip and corner tipping.

Figure 73

Circa 1885
size 24 by 40
Curved top design with crown frame is
three inches wide, inner liner burnished
gold, gold leaf, design similar to old kitchen
shaving mirror, but now designed for other
rooms.

are two basic types, red oak and white oak.

The red oak has an odd odor when it is freshly cut. The heartwood has a definite reddish tone with the sapwood leaning toward reddish brown. The wood is not as durable as the white oak and should not be used where they may be a condition for decay. Because of its inner structure the wood is not waterproof. If you were to make a barrel out of red oak it would leak.

The white oak heartwood is more of a light brown or tan color. The grain is of a finer texture with a softer appearance, whereas the red oak has a definitely coarser grain that is very predominant. Barrel making with white oak was and still is a big business.

Oak has always been a popular wood for furniture. Years ago, most of the furniture of the inexpensive variety was made out of oak and was naturally finished. The wood does take a nice finish, although the red oak has that wild grain. The white oak with an English oak finish was very popular during the 1800's. This was a rather dark walnut tone applied to the oak.

The wood has a large open grain and usually cannot be nailed without splitting. It is somewhat difficult to cut because of its hardness. Oak is very durable, has fair stability and it can be carved to a fair extent. The common 16 x 20 portrait frame of the late 1800's used oak extensively for the wood part of the multi-unit frame. The wood lends itself well to refinishing and without too much difficulty, one can easily restore a natural oak frame.

Maple

Maple is a heavy, strong wood that can take considerable wear. Although that property alone is not significant because you do not subject a frame to wear, the frame will last a long time. The wood has a very fine texture with a soft and beautiful grain. The wood has a close grain and does not require filling. The hard maple variety is used for cutting boards, maple furniture and also material that can be machined and turned.

Because of its hardness, maple is a difficult wood to use for picture frames. It has to be predrilled for every nail. The wood takes all types of stains and it can take a beautiful finish. It also has the property of taking a fine sheen when polished. Among the most important varieties of maples are the ones that give you a most unusual graining.

The tiger grain gives a striped appearance to the wood and it is much admired for its beauty. The application of the veneer of this wood goes back many years. The English used the veneer on the wood frames which they exported to the early American colonies.

The curly maple grain is somewhat similar except that instead of being striped, the grain has more of a curly nature. This grain was also valued for furniture. The Amish people, a religious group which centered around Pennsylvania and Ohio, were famous for their curly maple furniture. The maple takes on a beautiful patina as it gets older. The color approaches an amber tone and it has a very warm appeal.

Bird's eye maple is perhaps the most beautiful. Little marks resembling little eyes cover the surface at random (Figure 13). This type was also sought for veneering. The solid wood is difficult to machine because the grain runs in all directions. Stability in long strips is obviously low because of the grain formation. It is not exactly known why the grain takes on this formation.

One will sometimes find a tiger grain in other woods. This tiger marking is formed in the wood when the tree has twisted and bent in the wind, usually on the side of a mountain where the winds cause this motion.

Left Figure 74

Circa 1888
size 8 by 16
Three frame design, combination cylinder
compo and mold compo for finished corner
inner frame, gilt finish.

Right Figure 75

Circa 1890
size 16 by 24
Modified finish corner design mold compo,
separate liner.

Left Figure 76

Circa 1920
size 14 by 24
Example of simple design with minimum
compo, embellishments are mold compo,
small, wood frame dovetailed and covered
by means of the whiting box with template,
gold finish, had many types of paint finish.

XV – The General Designs Used in Compo Molding

Flowers, leaves and ferns have always been dominant in the compo designs. This was probably because nature is the aesthetic source of design. Since the beginning of time, true beauty has surrounded us. Even in the winter the snowflakes produced a barrage of delicate geometric designs. The ferns and leaves have a flowing design, with curved lines, while the snowflake creates a straight line formation. By adding to that the circle or half round formation, there was a storehouse of design elements upon which to draw. Early frames of French and Italian influence had a predominance of flowing designs.

When you hand-cut the fern and leaf design it can be undercut to your heart's content, but when you begin to use compo, you must consider that what you mold must be able to be released from that mold. This is the reason why compo is used. It is flexible when it is cast and can be readily released from the mold. The casting can also lay on the contoured surface and form into the design. If the design leans toward geometric or straight line designs then the influence is of more Asiatic feeling. The curved line design is accredited to the European flavor.

The middle 1800's showed a profusion of the oak leaf and acorn design (Figure 27). It seemed to be a popular figure to use. It gradually diminished around 1885.

Many other forms were used. The shield was popular in England, while the fleur-de-lis pattern was used on French frames. This particular pattern resembled three petals or floral segments of an iris tied by an encircling band.

XVI – Various Finishes Used on Old Frames

In order to begin to comprehend what finishes were used on the early picture frame, one must consider what materials were used. When it came to color, there were the pigment earths that were finely ground and the colored organic materials such as the juice of berries and barks, etc. In time the colored earths were refined into pure oxides of various minerals, which at that time were not recognized as such but were note for their respective color. The blue colors were from the cobalt bearing materials, while brown colors were from the iron oxides, green colors were from chrome bearing minerals, and copper bearing rocks and so on.

When it came to finding a vehicle to which these earths could be added, it was eventually discovered that certain oils had the right properties for accepting these finely ground earths. Linseed oil was found to be one of the best oils that could be used. It is a vegetable oil that is pressed from the seed of the flax plant. After the heating and filtering, the raw material is known as raw linseed oil. When heated to a higher temperature it becomes known as boiled linseed oil.

This combination of oil and pigment was to withstand time and is used even today. Chinawood oil was also used as a vehicle in varnishes. There were other combinations that were tried and some of them were good, but many proved fragile with time. There were artists who mixed egg albumen with pigments only to find that the elements caused the paint to deteriorate in time and flake off. Fish oil and other oils that could work were used, but while some were good, others failed to last.

Sealers and Finishes

When it came to a clear finish or sealer, there were many types to fill the bill. Shellac was found to be one of the best sealers. It also formed the base of some paints, made by mixing colored earths with the shellac. Oils of all types were used as sealers and finishes on wood.

Figure 77

Circa 1885
size 20 by 40
Six frame design, outer open network edging, all cylinder compo,
gilt finish.

Figure 78
Circa 1880
size 24 by 30
Four frame design, silver leaf in
pewter finish, also came in gilt
finish, frame slightly convex.

Figure 78a
inner frame, Circa 1880, 8 by 10
Three frame design, outer trim
custom formed, silver leaf finish,
inner trim natural oak, silver liner.

Figure 79

Circa 1910
size 14 by 28
Modified formed frame, finished
corners, compo embellishments,
gold leaf finish.

Oils eventually oxidize and form a hard and somewhat impervious coating. Some oils will oxidize more quickly than others. It was found that by boiling linseed oil, the oxidation process was faster when exposed to air. Much of the furniture of the early was finished with an oil finish. Even today many Europeans will only accept an oil finish on their furniture. Many fine pieces of furniture that have long been in the family have only an oil finish applied and when it was time to rejuvenate the piece it was merely washed and another coat of oil was applied. The same procedure was used for picture frames and mirrors.

Resins

There were also resins that were used for a clear type of finish. In time it was found that by mixing the resin with oils, a different type of material was made. This was the beginning of varnishes. In general, varnish consists of copal gums, resins, linseed oil and turpentine.

The development of varnish was a gradual one. The varnish of today differs from what was created prior to the 20th century. Varnish that contained a larger proportion of oil to the gum, became later known as a long oil varnish. It had the properties of being a slower drying material and it was somewhat softer. The material was more durable. Varnish that has a larger proportion of gums was known as a short oil type of varnish. The material dried faster but was somewhat brittle. However, the varnish could be sanded easier.

Solvents

Solvents also formed an important part of varnishes and oil finishes. The most common types were turpentine and alcohol. Turpentine was derived from certain trees and was extensively used by the artist who mixed the colored earths, oils and turpentine. This was the material he painted with. The turpentine would evaporate leaving the pigment and oil to harden by oxidation. There were times when the artist would forget to add enough linseed oil while making paint and instead would use only turpentine and pigment. The result of this mistake was a finish that would not hold up and would merely flake off in time.

Alcohol was used mainly as a shellac solvent. The solvent would evaporate leaving only the shellac and whatever pigment was added to it. Naphtha and benzene were solvents, and they were used also, especially in later periods. They were derived from coal tar and petroleum.

Texturizers

Another medium was used for a base as well as a texturizer. This material is called gesso. It has the consistency of a thick paste and was made by combining whiting with water and then adding boiled linseed oil and animal glue. This mixture was heated together and the result was a texturizing paste that could be used to stipple or even create a carved effect on wood. Colors could be added to the mixture. Early artists used this mixture for the treatment of some of the crude border-like frames on church paintings. This material is used even today. With a slight modification of the formula you have the material called compo which was used to mold the dimensional trim on frames.

Gesso Preparation

Mix whiting or powdered chalk with water to a thick cream consistency. Then pour into a double boiler that has a mixture of 4 parts linseed oil and 6 parts animal glue. Heat over a slow flame for about 10-12 minutes. Then place in a jar or container and seal until used. The material can be applied by brush and stippled or treated in various ways to create the finishes desired.

Figure 80
Circa 1895
size 16 by 20
Four frames, basswood toned with stain, typical
portrait frame.

Figure 81
Circa 1895
size 16 by 20
Four frames, oak with compo inlay, gold on
cylinder compo, gold liner.

Figure 82
Circa 1880
size 8 by 17 custom
Deep European gold frame.

Figure 83
Circa 1895
size 16 by 20
Plain oak edge, four frame design, portrait
frame.
Figure 84 (inner frame)
Circa 1880
size 8 by 10
Walnut edge carved with liner.

Figure 85
Circa 1898
size 16 by 20
Four inches wide, gilt finish, give away type,
yellow pine base with rolled compo by cylinder.

Compo Preparation

For a four pound mix, use the following formula:

1 lb. flake carpenter glue
1 lb. yellow rosin lump
1 qt. water
¼ pt. linseed oil
2 lb. whiting

Dissolve the glue in the water and heat over a double boiler. Melt the rosin in a double boiler and add the linseed oil. To this mixture add the water mixture, then slowly add the whiting until it becomes like putty. Use the mixture while still freshly made. The mixture has little self life, although it can be softened again by heating over a steam table. The compo will dry in about 24 hours depending on the thickness and the type of mix you have.

No one knows who discovered the formula for compo but it was used as far back as 1200 A.D. and probably even earlier. The material has a very long life because it eventually hardens into a fossil-like form. It does become brittle but this depends upon the original mixture. There are many variations of the formula and each artisan will add his own touch. I know of one fellow who would add one-half roll of toilet paper to the above mixture to give it binding quality.

Wood Stains

Very early stains were derived from organic sources. The bark and wood from certain trees after being steam-distilled would produce stains that were used to stain other woods. The colors would usually be in the brown range. Plants would produce a host of colors that would range in the blues, violets, reds, greens and almost every color in the rainbow. There were also berries that would produce desired stains. I am sure that we are all familiar with what a nice stain blueberries can give. Oxides of metals in earths and other metallic salts gave colors that were used to stain woods.

Aniline, which is a coal tar derivative, formed one of the bases for the 19th century stains. It is a material that is slightly soluble in water and also soluble in organic solvents such as alcohol. It was first prepared in 1826 as one of the products obtained by heating indigo to a high temperature. Since the material came from the indigo plant, it was called aniline because the Sanskrit word for the plant is "nila" and the specific name derived from that is "anil".

In 1856, Sir William Perkin treated aniline with potassium dichromate and obtained a violet-colored material which could be used as a dye. Eventually the material was made from the benzene obtained from coal tar and petroleum. This dye added to the growing lists of stains that were used to stain wood.

Stains came in many forms. The list below gives some of their characteristics.

Water Stains

Water stains are non-fading and brilliant. They have a deep penetration and they are quite uniform. One disadvantage is that the grain of the wood is raised and must be sanded in order to level it.

Spirit Stains

These stains are made with powder that is dissolved in a solvent such as alcohol. The aniline dyes fit this category. They dried very rapidly but they had a tendency to bleed through almost any finish that was applied over them. Many of the colors will fade quickly unless they are protected with many coats of finish.

Pigment Oil Stains

Pigment oil stains are made by mixing very finely ground pigments with linseed oil and turpentine or other solvents. The colors are very stable and do not bleed, but they do have the tendency to cover some of the grain of the wood.

Penetrating Oil Stains

Powder stains are dissolved in solvents such as benzene or turpentine in order to produce a penetrating stain. The colors are fairly stable and they have one advantage over a water stain in that they do not raise the wood grain. They are bleeding colors but this can be corrected by sealing them with shellac.

Most of the above stains were used in the pre-Revolutionary periods and they are still in use today. While we have added to the inventory of stains and have introduced other techniques of application, the basics of all staining came centuries ago.

Shellac, the Master Sealer

Shellac is a natural resin which is secreted by a scale insect, LACCIFER LACCA, which lives on the twigs of certain trees native to India and the East Indies. The resin is collected, dried and purified to make the various grades. Shellac is available as flakes, which can be dissolved in alcohol, and also is manufactured in a ready-to-use form. In the ready-to-use form it comes as a four or six pound cut, which means that the shellac has been cut with alcohol and each gallon contains a certain quantity of shellac. A four pound cut means that there is four pounds of shellac in one gallon of alcohol. In use the shellac is further cut with alcohol by 30 to 50%. The material dries through the evaporation of the solvent.

Shellac has remarkable qualities. Oil paints and resin varnishes use naphtha and turpentine as thinners, while lacquers use a lacquer thinner, but shellac uses alcohol as its solvent. You can use shellac over any finish which you could not do with the lacquers. It can be applied coat after coat and can be sanded between coats in a short time. It takes only about twenty minutes to dry. Colors can be added to the shellac. Black lacquerware uses a refined form of shellac and lampblack.

Early wood finishes used shellac as a finish. Each coat was wiped on and sanded until a sufficient cover was built up. It could be easily sanded even after fifty years. The color of natural shellac is an amber orange, although the shellac does have a tendency to turn darker when exposed to air. Most of the white shellac used today is a synthetic shellac. All leafing today would have a harsh finish if it were not for shellac. The material gives the surface a patina that is amber-toned and as a barrier against bleeding colors it is unexcelled.

Gilt Finish on Old Finishes

Regardless what any manufacturer will say, there has never been or ever will be a gilt finish that will look exactly like gold leaf after a simple paint application. Gilt finish is made with powdered bronze, whereas the gold leaf or metal leaf is whole metal. The two differ in physical appearance and simply cannot be made to look alike. Gilt paint is made of two components, the bronze powder and a vehicle in which the powder is suspended. Since the bronzing powder is heavy it has a tendency to settle quickly, so that you have to mix it very often while it is being used. The method of creating powdered bronze had been known for some time but the vehicle that it was added to had been a problem in the 1800's. Much experimentation took place and I have found finishes that are over 100 years old and still have not hardened. You can take your finger nail and scrape them right off. Banana oil was a vehicle that proved effective and was used for a long time.

Gilt paint has a few drawbacks, one of them that the gilt finish will change color after a while. Most of the gilt finishes today are on the soft side. This can make it difficult to tone with toners because it has a tendency to dissolve some of the gilt finish. The same problem occurred in early finishes. Today this has been solved by using lacquer base gilt paint. Lacquer gilt paint has to be made fresh and then used that same day because it has a tendency to gel and become useless.

There was a time when it was almost impossible to make a silver paint using powdered aluminum until it was found that by treating the aluminum powder with stearic acid, the aluminum was able to remain suspended in the vehicle for a longer time rather than simply sinking to the bottom like a rock.

Most of the old gilt finishes can be touched up with the current gilt paint available. There is a host of color variations to the bronzing powders. Each color variation is created by the ratio of different metals in the making of the bronze powder. It can vary from a light gold to a deep copper or bronze. The color of Roman gold is one shade used well on the old frames.

Tortoise Shell Finish

Tortoise shell is derived from the horny plates of the hawk-billed turtle. By means of heat and pressure the plates are flattened. Boulle work is a highly decorative form of inlay which utilized brass or silver and tortoise shell. This form of art was developed by Andre Charles Boulle (1642-1732).

Many fine pieces of furniture and early frame (Figure C) exhibited tortoise shell. The Louis XIII to Louis XVI periods were to display many fine desk chests and other pieces that were inlaid with the multi-colored tortoise shell. It was therefore inevitable that someone would try to imitate tortoise shell in a finish. It is suspected that the following technique was used: The surface was primed with a base color, then thinned drops of coloring was dropped on the surface, using a feather to move the colors about (Figure 4). Other variations were applying colors to the feather and impressing the surface.

This finish was expanded to include many variations. It was the basis of many types of finishes that were to appear in the 1800's. The simulated finish was to fall into two categories, the tortoise shell and its related styles, and the simulated wood grain finish.

Variations of the tortoise shell finish were to include not only the multicolor applications but also one color speckled or mottled finish. This was done by applying one color on a base color frame with a sponge or wad of cloth. Depending on how the applicator was used, many different effects could be created. The artisan could overlay one color on top of another and make variations. The final product was sealed in shellac and rubbed. This type of finish was extensively used in the mid 1800's and formed one of the liners of a type of frames that were composed of many frames assembled together.

The other variation was the simulated wood grain effect. This type of finish took on particular importance in simulating woods that were more costly. The finish also allowed the use of a wood grain panel in multi-paneled moulding. One could have a simulated outer edge of wood, then a black stripe, a speckled section, another black stripe, an inset panel of simulated wood grain and finally a gold leaf lip. The combinations were of infinite number. Later, around 1900, the wood grain effect was to be the dominant finish on frames because it was simple to apply in the manner used in 1900. The painstaking care of true graining was beginning to disappear. The first wood grain to appear was so fine that it was difficult to see that it was not the true wood grain. Later the work became more coarse and by 1900 it was nothing more than a brush movement across the surface with a suitable color. By 1910, frames were being produced with a cross grain finish and then edged in black.

Toning Frames

A large portion of frames that are leafed are then toned with a glaze or gesso mixture. The gesso was mixed with raw umber, burnt umber, or other pigments, applied to the leafed surface and wiped off. This left a residue in the niches of the design and a slight film over the surface. The material gave the surface a mellow tone and simulated age. Today we also use a compound called glaze in which the pigments are added and applied in the same manner as gesso.

XVII — The Picture Frame Today

I classify all frames made prior to 1900 as antique frames. The reason for the 1900 date is that prior to that time, the very fine frames were created. About 1900 a complete transition of frame design began, and manufacturing of frames was in full swing. Simplicity of design was beginning to become dominant and the beautiful Victorian frame was disappearing. Modernism was coming into being, revealed slowly at first, and really beginning to accelerate after World War I. Furniture and accessories were going to a modern decor and the picture frame also went in that direction. Just as wide frames had appeared in the 19th century, the narrow frame now appeared in the 20th century. Compo moulding use was at a minimum and casting of entire frame faces took place, all with minimal design in order to control costs.

In the early 1900's, a process of creating frames by a mold process was extensively used. This involved the following procedure: A cavity large enough to become the size of the frame was made and into this cavity a strong gelatin or glue solution was poured. A frame or model was placed into this solution with the face side down and just below the surface. This was allowed to set up and cool. Finally the frame was removed leaving a mold of the frame. In order to make frames from this mold, a thin compo solution of a specific formula (generally a guarded trade secret), was poured into this cavity, and then a wood form which was to become the backbone of the frame, was pressed into this solution. The excess would spill over and the mold was allowed to set. After a certain period, the frame was removed from the gelatin mold. A number of frames were made from the same mold. If it became unusable, one simply melted the gelatin mold and poured it back into the cavity. He then would take one of the frames made and sank it into the solution. This would create another mold. This process is amazingly similar to the latex mold process that is used today, where a latex solution covers an object or frame and then is allowed to cure. When it has cured, you have a mold in which you can create a frame or whatever.

There were also metal molds created to make small picture frames. These molds were made of bronze, lead, or a combination of both. They were more durable, but they did not have the flexibility of the gelatin mold. The mold had to have a release taper included in the design so that the mold could be removed from the frame. In some cases a thin wire was sunk into the compo to facilitate pulling it out of the mold. Plaster of Paris was sometimes used when the entire molded object contained no wood in it. This material can never be used by itself on wood frames as it is sometimes assumed, because Plaster of Paris does not stick to wood without the addition of a glue of some type.

Framed picture units were now really making their appearance. Department stores and Woolworth's 5 and 10 were just some of the many outlets. One could purchase small pictures, nostalgic sayings, and words of wisdom from 10¢ to a dollar at Woolworth's. The frames were of a very thin stock measuring about three-eighths of an inch by one-half inch, and were held together by one nail in each corner.

From 1915 until just recently, the frames for the most part were nondescript. They were stripped of the compo trim, the fine gold leaf, the burnished gold lips, the fine wood graining and the multiple finishes. During this period, the frames drifted into an era of gilt finish and color stripping.

However, in Europe the art of fine compo frames did not disappear. Even back in 1870, large compo moulding was imported from Europe just as it is today. There are a limited number of American companies that will produce some compo frames, but the countries of France, Italy, Sweden and Belgium are the main sources. After World War II, there began a return to fine frame moulding. In the thirties many people removed that fine frame around their favorite painting, and reframed the painting with the vogue moulding of that day. Later, they were to realize that something was lost in the painting, but by this time, the original frame was either destroyed or put into the attic.

XVIII — The Use of Antique Frames

The first picture frames that were used were simple flat frames. Each was used merely for housing a painting and no emphasis was placed on it. Around 1200 A.D., the frame began to show prominence. We were evolving from the stagnant dark ages and the frame was beginning to blossom as was the art that it contained. As art developed, so did the frame. It grew from the simple wood structure to the Barbizon frame, the Rococo frame, the ebony wood carved frame and other dimensionally ornate designs.

One can follow the construction of the frame by going to a large art museum and observing the types of frames that originally came with the early works of art. Someday when you go to your local museum, I would suggest that you concentrate on the frame part of the paintings. A whole new set of concepts will open up to you. In many cases there was more work involved in the making of the frame than there was in the work of art which it contained. Many of the works of art were conceived in two or three days, but the frame that housed it could have taken two months to create.

There is a tendency on the part of some artists to use a most unusual baroque frame for their creation because they are unsure of their own work. Therefore, to sustain interest and emphasis on their creations, they house them in magnificent frames. It is a basic fact that a good painting can look poor in a poor frame, and a poor painting can be made to look good in a fine frame. Many artists make the fatal mistake of housing their creations in as inexpensive frames as possible mainly because of the cost factor. They do not realize that the frame reflects on their work. Some artists only see their works and are oblivious to the frame. The buyer on the other hand, observes the painting **and the frame!** After all, both are to hang in the home of the buyer. The artist must be made to realize that he or she is really in business when they are selling their merchandise. Therefore since this is true, does it not seem proper to house their commodity in the best possible package? Putting it bluntly, you are not going to put a Mona Lisa into a frame made of wood slats or orange crates and expect someone who is capable of paying you a thousand dollars or so for it, to buy it and to say the least, hang it in their $50,000 home. They are many paintings created by artists

Figure 86

Circa 1890
size 10 by 12
Four frame design Ebony oak finish, silver leaf cylinder compo.

Figure 87

Circa 1865
size 11 by 15
Outer frame walnut. Inner frame walnut in four pieces with oval opening, carved designs in corners, gold leaf lip.

Figure 88

Circa 1890
size approx. 8 by 10
English oak with gold leaf cylinder compo, the frame is eight inches in width.

that are housed in frames which the artists themselves would not even think to hang in their own homes.

The fashion trend has always been a factor in deciding what kind of frame design went in the home. In early Europe and England, the fashions of clothing and furniture were to reach new highs in "fanciness." Turnings and intricate works were both used to reach new proportions and the picture frame joined in this trend. The 17th, 18th, and 19th centuries produced a predominance of baroque and intricate frames.

Young America copied Europe insofar as house furnishings and clothing were concerned and although we were to some extent, "primitive and backwoodsy," we still followed the old country in taste. However, our home designs differed in the Colonial period, because we **were** backwoodsy and Colonial. Our homes were constructed of local lumber with the crudest of manufacture. We have to remember that America is really a very young country by European standards. A piece of furniture that is one hundred years old here is considered an antique, but in Europe it would be considered recent. The same rule applies to picture frames. Our Colonial character was reflected in some of the frames we used. In America we recognize a certain period that is called the Colonial period and because of the great abundance of wood that we had, there was bound to be an effect on what the motif of homes in America would be.

Pine was the dominant wood that was used, but it was actually unsuitable for frames. Cherry, maple, walnut and oak were the other dominant woods of America. These hardwoods were suitable for picture frame moulding. Walnut proved to be the most usable and the most beautiful. It could be shaped easily, nailed readily, and finished beautifully in its natural finish. The carving of the wood was easily done. There is a frame of walnut, called the cross frame, which had an embellishment of a carved piece of walnut at each intersection. The frame was hand carved and formed a cross at each corner (Figure 12). Observe the westerns on television and you will always see the cross frame hanging in the room background. This frame is currently desired for the needlepoints that are made today. The walnut frame in combination with a tortoise shell or a gold liner, was to be a dominant combination in the late 1800's. This wood was later to be imitated in a simulated finish. It takes a watchful eye to detect a simulated walnut finish, but an experienced person can do so.

There are some basic guidelines followed in the selection of frames for the subject matter. The rule is to always complement the subject matter first. The basic purpose of the picture frame is to house and enhance what the frame contains. Some interior decorators will incorporate the color of the sofa in the liner of the frame, or perhaps they will tint the frame with the same color of the drapes. In this process they completely forget or ignore what the addition will do to the painting itself. The handling of antique frames in the homes by some interior decorators is limited simply because they have so little experience in that phase of work.

Antique frames can be made to fit almost any decor, but they do have to be handled individually with each case. Take for example, modern impressionistic art. After separating the subject from the frame by the use of a mat or liner, one can use a very baroque frame with much detail, but the color or texture of the frame must be completely subdued by painting it totally black, brown, or some other desired flat color. This is so that it is evident that the detail does exist there, but the detail should not hit you in the eye. A painting of flowers or some subject matter that has great detail and is called "busy," should have a subdued wood frame with a liner of great interest, or a busy frame **provided** that a suitable liner or mat is used to separate the subject from the frame. There has to be a separation by a blank area or else it will appear as one confused mass.

Landscapes lend themselves well to fine antique frames. They can be housed in either baroque or simple frames. Here is a case where the motif of the room can be tied to the frame. The landscape can fit almost any room in the home. If the motif is Spanish, contemporary, Italian, etc., a landscape can fit that area with the frame that would reflect the motif. There are antique frames that will fit any decor.

Frames of the English Period

The English period effect can be carried through by wood veneer, simulated wood grain, a simple dark wood frame with a gold leaf liner, a muted baroque frame of gold or the simple burnished gold leaf frames. Unlike the continental frames which were basically heavy and dimensionally impressive, the English frames leaned toward the filigree and shield designs. The frames were intricate with repetitive details. Many of the early colonial frames came from England and hence, the maple veneer and the burnished gold frames were representations of the English taste. The tortoise combinations which basically leaned toward a simulated wood grain were also used. (Figures 1, 2, 5, 10, 13, 14, 17, 31, 50, 51, 62, 63, 64, 72, 73, 75, 79, 87, 89), color (Figures C-1, 4, 5, 8, 14, 15, 17, 19, 20, 21, 22, 23, 26.)

The Country French Effect

The Country French effect or touch can be fulfilled by distressed wood frames with pewter liners of an ornate nature. Some tortoise frames will add an interest also. Walnut frames can fit this period as well as most of the colonial frames. "Country-French" is a term that is used for the French farm influence. There is also such a relationship to our own farm influence. The farm relates to the homestead, the homestead relates to the settlers, and the settlers relate to the Colonial period. (Figures 1, 2, 4, 5, 10, 11, 13, 14, 17, 21, 25, 26, 28, 31, 33, 34, 50, 51, 52, 53, 62, 63, 65, 80, 81, 83, 86, 87, 89, 98, 107), color (Figures C-2, 8, 11, 13, 14, 17, 19, 20, 21, 22, 23, 25, 26, 28, 29, 30.)

The Mediterranean or Spanish Influence

This motif can be observed with massive pewter or silver leaf frames, or wood frames with silver or gold liners, and certain wide gold frames. The Moorish influence is apparent in the design, and because of this, the frames have a flavor unlike the Italian or French frames. Many of the frames of the 1870 period were from five to eight inches in width. The use of velvet can be present although velvet was used as far back as 1200. Velvet generally does not last beyond 75 years because it deteriorates. I have seen velvet on frames that are 700 years old, but it could have been that the velvet was redone. If the velvet is in bad condition it can be replaced without a great effort.

Although silver is the dominant color, one can also use gold. The distressed frame also fits this period. This type of frame is especially desirable and the antique ones are really rare. Frames that exhibit carvings can also fit under this heading. However, the moderately carved frame is more a product of a later period such as around 1920 or so. The Mexican carved frame is, of course, of recent vintage. (Figures 3, 7, 9, 17, 20, 23, 25, 30, 68, 69, 70, 78, 81, 86, 90, 101, 104, 105), color (Figures C-2, 3, 6, 14, 15, 20, 24, 25, 27, 29.)

Contemporary Feel

The contemporary touch is perhaps the most common of the decors today. This feeling can be expanded into two categories. The first is a formal contemporary which can call for baroque frames, while the other is an informal contemporary which allows tiffany finishes, umber tone finishes and almost any frame type for accent. "Contemporary" is a catch-all term which really means that it has no real label for a motif, but it signifies a home with furniture that is comfortable and can be mixed in furnishings. It may include a touch of modern here, and a colonial touch there, but nothing that appears in quantity to indicate a specific period. (Figures 6, 10, 17, 24, 29, 36, 37, 43, 44, 47, 50, 51, 52, 53, 54, 56, 60, 61, 72, 73, 75, 76, 79, 87, 94, 96, 102, 103), color (Figures C-4, 15, 21, 22.)

The French Period

The French period will always indicate a Rococo or a Barbizon type of frame. Since the French took the Italian frame and embellished it further, the only result could be a frame of flamboyancy or of intricate flowing line structures. The French frames are beyond a shadow of a doubt, "busy." The local art museum will quickly show how the French artists utilized the frames that housed their creations. The rules for separation of a busy painting and a busy frame with a plain liner still applied. The types of Barbizon frame that were used in the 1800's are the frames that we would be most acquainted with. This style of frame still exists today. The Barbizon frame was one that was adaptable to the compo mold. The Rococo frame was difficult to produce from the mold because of the undercuts that were present. The Barbizon type of frame could be produced from molds and because the demand for this type of frame was increasing, it was the logical style to take over. It was in reality, a small example of the effect that mass production would have on a commodity even at that early date. (Figures 8, 18, 19, 20, 22, 24, 27, 29, 36, 37, 41, 42, 43, 44, 45, 46, 48, 49, 58, 61, 68, 71, 74, 95, 99, 100, 106), color (Figures C-5, 9, 22, 27.)

The Italian Period

As we have noted in the first chapter of this book, the Italian school of frames relied on heavy scroll and compo work. There is a definite relationship between the Italian and French frames because the French utilized the designs of the Italians and carried them on from there. For an Italian motif, you could use many of the French frames plus certain types that seemed to still have an Italian feeling. The very early influences of Italian frames would have that character. (Figures 2, 10, 16, 19, 22, 27, 29, 30, 41, 42, 45, 46, 47, 48, 49, 65, 70, 73, 87, 90, 106), color (Figures C-1, 5, 7, 8, 9, 10, 21, 22, 27, 30.)

The Colonial Period

Country French and Colonial motifs are very similar. The early colonies could be reflected by primitive frames and simple tortoise frames. There was also the very early simple gold frame that was predominant in England during the Revolutionary period. Wood frames such as walnut would have their place in this period. (Figures 13, 24, 25, 26, 50, 51, 84, 87), color (Figures C-8, 11, 13, 15, 16, 17, 21, 22, 26.)

The Victorian Period

The Victorian type of furniture and its related items are just beginning to be recognized and they have not reached their full potential since the period was one of heaviness in both frames and furniture. The oak pieces were massive and not really attractive to many people. With the surge of antique buying, it seems that these pieces are now disappearing. Once they almost completely disappear, there will be a demand for that motif and the Victorian period will have arrived. Since most of the frames listed in the book have come from that period, you can assume that you may use a large portion of them. The following list is for the frames that reflect this period more than others. (Figures 4, 5, 6, 29, 35, 44, 46, 56, 60, 66, 70, 77, 80, 81, 85, 86, 88, 97, 106, 107), color (Figures C-1, 2, 3, 4, 5, 7, 10, 12, 18, 20, 22a, 23, 25, 26, 27.)

Regardless what the motif of the rooms are, it is perfectly proper to have an occasional antique frame in the room. One frame in a modern setting retains the connection of the past with the trend of the future. By nature the old frames were very wide, and because of this some feel

MINIATURE FRAMES

Figure 89

Circa 1870
size 2 by 4
Matched pair, curly maple outer frame, tortoise second frame, gold leaf liner.

Figures 90-91

Circa 1880
size 4 by 4
Both frames silver leaf on cylinder compo design.

Figure 92

Circa 1874
size 6 by 8
Delicate fine scalloped compo, all hand cut out network, gold leaf with black toning.

Figure 93

Circa 1895
size 4 by 6
Outer frame oak, inner liner silver leaf.

Figure 94

Circa 1898
size 4 by 6
Matched pair cylinder compo stick moulding, tiffany finish.

that many of the frames have a tendency to overpower the subject matter. This can be true, but it depends upon the structure of the frame. Some parts of the frame design can replace what a mat is generally intended to do, to separate the subject matter from the frame.

There are many cases where a certain picture is to be placed in a certain room, and yet no matter what frame is placed on the picture, there seems to be a clash of the picture and the room. This is probably a case where the picture simply does not fit the room. Some pictures are stereotyped for certain areas of the home. For example, fruit pictures usually fit the dining room area or the kitchen area. Nudes are generally destined for the bedroom or the bathroom.

XIX — Repairing Antique Frames

The elements take a toll on picture frames. Unless great care is taken to preserve old frames, they will simply fall apart. Many frames have long been stored in attics where they are subjected to extreme conditions of heat and cold. The conditions in the attics are such that the humidity is extremely low. This has quite an effect on the wood and compo. Frames stored in a barn would receive the same treatment. In many cases these frames would be stored in the attic or barn for perhaps thirty years or so. Every winter there would be extreme cold on the frame and when summer came, they would be subjected to temperatures of up to perhaps 115 degrees.

Frames stored in the basement would be exposed to a different destructive force, moisture. This can swell the frames, thus cracking the compo and eventually disintegrating it.

If the frames actually come in direct contact with moisture, such as from a flood in the basement, then the compo will turn to powder. Exposure to moisture need not be long before it would distintegrate. This is why great care must be taken when washing picture frames.

During my travels in search of frames, I have seen thousands of frames that have been destroyed by water. I recall one time a basement of a shop that had recently had a fire on the first floor. Inside there were stored over one thousand old frames that had been removed from pictures during the early twenties when people replaced them with vogue frames of that period. The fire had been put out but the water from that fire saturated everything in the basement. Had the frames been removed immediately, there would have been very little loss. Since the frames were not recognized as valuable at that time, they were simply forgotten and the frames remained soaked in the damp basement with no air coming into the room. Later, I was to see the results. There were row after row of frames completely stripped of compo and covered with a black mildew. They were still wet from the fire. You could see the remains of fine early 19th century ovals and Barbizon frames. There were massive ones and even some that were actually hand carved, which indicated that they came from even an earlier period. It was a distressing sight.

Most of the frames of the 1800's will need some work. The types of repair can be many and I will itemize and discuss each type of repair that you generally will run into.

Hairline Cracks in the Compo

This is not a detrimental feature on an old frame. You must remember that it took perhaps fifty years to create those cracks. I suggest you do nothing about them because they show character. To prevent further cracking, I would suggest that the entire frame be given a spray coat of sealer, after the frame has been repaired or cleaned if needed.

Pieces Missing in the Compo Work

You will hear many people tell you of the many ways that you can recreate the missing parts or repair what is missing on the frame. I have heard of people using chewing gum on the frame, forming the contours and allowing it to dry. To me it always looked like a piece of gum stuck on a picture frame. Some people will use plaster and just fill up the missing area. This is crude and it is really obvious that it has been filled. The only way that you can do a good job is to make a cast of a similar section and make a casting. This cast can be made of plaster of paris. You can cut and fit the piece in and with the use of white glue and spackle, it can be sealed in place. This will involve time but it will be worth it.

One of the most difficult repairs to make is the thin filigree compo. This is difficult to cast because it is very thin. In this case you can cover the area with a thin spackle coat and draw, by means of a nail or such, the design needed.

Repair of Open Corners in a Wood Frame

In order to repair the corner, the frame must be evaluated to find what approach to use. Old antique frames will have nails in them that may have rusted in the wood. If the decision is to recut the miters for a better fit, the frame will have to be taken apart, with nails removed, and then recut. Sometimes the nail removal will cause further damage to the frame. Judgment must be made as to the feasibility of taking the frame apart.

Sometimes, when the frame is opened up, a long standing stress within the frame is released and this will prove difficult to re-assemble even though the miters are perfectly cut. If possible, reuse the original nails after straightening them.

The other approach is to fill the corner with spackle and then tone the filling in with suitable stains. This is done more frequently than taking the frame apart because it is easier. Yet it is necessarily better. In staining the wood, be careful not to use a stain that is too dark for the frame because the spackle has a tendency to take on a darker look. After staining, give the area a shellac wipe in order to seal the surface.

Repair of Open Corners in a Compo Covered Frame

This type of repair is easier than on a natural wood frame. If the frame requires pieces that are missing, then you must cast them and install the parts, but if the corner is just open, the following procedure is necessary.

First, force white glue between the joint and wipe off the excess. Then take the spackle and wipe smoothly over the joint. A wet rag may help in smoothing the spackle and keep the area covered with it at a minimum. Remember, wherever the spackle remains, that area has to be later toned in.

After the spackle has air dried, take some shellac and coat the raw spackle surface. By the use of either the gilt paint or the toners which are proper for the frame, then proceed to tone in the repaired section of the frame. Whenever you apply gold paint to an old surface, the area looks brand new. This appearance is not desired, so you have to "dirty" or age the gilt finish. This can be done with burnt umber, in a glaze, or with walnut stain that has been wiped on and wiped off after a short time or other toners that can be prepared to remove the newness of the paint. As to which one specifically to use, I cannot say without seeing the frame, but these hints will be of help in guiding you.

Stripping the Compo Off Old Frames

Sometimes the frame is in such a condition that it is economically unfeasible to repair. This does not mean that the frame is totally useless.

It is possible to strip all the compo off the frame and end up with a very fine piece that will be an excellent primitive frame. The stripped frame may expose a most unusual texture or grain. To strip the frame, use the following procedures.

There are two approaches to stripping the compo off the frame. The first way is to soak the frame in a bathtub or suitable container where it can be covered with water and allowed to set. If the family can manage living together for about two weeks without a bath, the bathtub is the best place. The material will gradually fall apart or can be scraped off, but it is important that there be no forced scraping of the surface or damage will occur to the frame. Use steel wire brushes for this purpose. A table knife or some dull instrument can aid removal, but you cannot hurry the process. It has to be done at its own speed, not yours.

The second way is to put the frame on the roof or any place where the elements can get to the frame. It is preferable that the frame be placed where it will remain soaked longer. Dependent on conditions, it may take up to three months to remove the material from the frame. I use this process because there is little handling involved and there is also no gouging of the frame. I have a flat roof and the frames lay there getting both soaked and snowed upon. The freezing also helps to remove the old compo. After removal, wash the frame and allow it to dry. In both cases the number of usable frames to come out of stripping will probably be one out of three, because in some cases there were open knots that were filled by the compo during the making of the stick moulding or the water may twist the frame out of proportion. Another probability is that the frame will fall apart if the glue holding the frame together has been leached out of the frame. There are many other conditions that will occur that could render the frame unusable.

The ovals are really nice when you have stripped them down to the bare wood, but be prepared to reglue all the parts of the oval back together again. Be sure to number the backs with a marker so that you will rejoin the same pieces again.

After the frame has thoroughly dried, you should reset all the nails, since the expansion of the frame will have pulled them out somewhat. The next step is to refinish the frame. If you simply apply shellac and hand rub the frame down, you may be pleased with that result.

You may find it more interesting if you sand the frame, apply a wash coat of shellac, and allow it to dry, then wipe a stain of walnut or fruitwood on the frame and seal that stain again when it is dry with shellac. Finally, after steel wool sanding apply a good paste wax on the frame and it is done. The staining will give the frame an aged patina that is more interesting than the raw wood shellacked and sealed.

Through the artful use of an original gold liner with the stripped frame, you create one of the finest of primitive frames, most suitable for early American pieces, Mediterranean feelings, primitive works of art and the country French motif. The frame is highly prized because of its usual appearance and rarity. You can understand why the frame is rare because of the work involved in the creation of the frame. The woods most suitable for this process are basswood and pine. Although oak was used for compo coverage it had a greater tendency to warp in the process of stripping.

Repair of Silver Leaf Frames

The repair of silver leaf frames is similar to gold leaf except a different color has to be contended with. Aluminum paint can tone some areas in, but if the area is large, then the entire frame should be releafed in silver or aluminum. The toning for the frame leans toward the black side and a black glaze generally helps tone the repair into the frame.

Figure 95

Circa 1895
size 14 by 19
Cast white metal, brass coated, delicate
design.

Figure 96

Circa 1900
size 14 by 20
Oblong with curved corners, base frame
four part dovetail, cream base with gilt
tipping.

Left Figure 97

Circa 1888
size 16 by 20
Four piece design, outer frame compo with
corner ornaments, ribbed oak frame, gold
leaf liner, compo inner liner.

Figure 98

Circa 1885
Various examples of tortoise shell frames with assorted liners
of the time.

Repair of Velvet on Old Frames

Velvet on the old frames lasts about fifty years. After that the velvet simply disintegrates. Sometimes the velvet, because of its partial disintegration, has an individual beauty of its own. With a light sealer coat of lacquer it is possible to retain that beauty. If the velvet is in poor shape, then it is possible to replace it.

The colors most generally used in the 1800's were black and red or maroon. The velvet was applied using animal glue which is soluble in water. The method of removal is to detach the velvet liner and soak it in hot water. Eventually the old velvet will come off easily. Be sure to remove all residue of the old glue. After drying, cut 1½ inch strips of velvet to the approximate length of the sides. With the use of some current spray adhesives, apply each strip to the liner while using care in the contour cutting of the corners. Since you are replacing the velvet you have the opportunity to add a velvet color which could coincide with the room motif.

Repair of Tortoise Shell Finishes

This finish can be the most difficult finish to repair. It is difficult, if not impossible to recreate the original finish. You may try to fake the repair by filling in the area with spackle and toning the area with colors already present there. The toning of the areas usually cannot be noticed if it is expertly done. There is usually a predominance of black edging which can cover a lot of repair.

Cleaning Walnut Frames

In restoring walnut frames, the usual problems are cleaning the walnut and repairing the gold liners. First, remove the liner and clean the walnut by scrubbing the wood with a strong soap and water. Do not allow the frame to be soaked for too long a period. If there are scratches or mars on the walnut, many of these can be subdued by wiping the frame with a walnut stain and then wiping off all excess. After a light steel wool rubbing with a fine grade steel wool, you may, if you desire, spray it with a coat of a lacquer sealer. The liner can be touched up, but if there are pieces of the liner missing, then they will have to be filled and repaired. It is difficult to specify exactly what to do unless the exact conditions are known.

Cleaning Gilt Finish Frames

For the most part, frames get a quick washing with a sudsy soap solution, and this, with a quick rinse and finally a quick drying, will generally do a good job of cleaning. You can touch up the gold with a gold paint. The color usually used is called Roman gold. After applying this touchup, it would be best to wipe over the new touchup with a slight glaze solution to kill the newness of the touchup. It could be advisable to spray the entire frame with a sealer which will brighten up the entire frame.

Repair of Gold Leaf Frames

Where there are broken sections on the frame, these have to be formed and filled with spackle. Try not to interfere with the remaining sections of the frame that are in good shape. Each repair is a separate problem and where there is a large area (over one inch), then it is difficult to repair without being noticeable. Most small repair jobs can be finished and toned in with Roman gold gilt. If the repair is extensive then a complete metal leafing will be needed.

Repair of Combination Wood and Gold Frames

Perhaps one of the most common frames of the late 1800's was the combination wood and gold frame. This frame was constructed of four frames, with the basic size being 16 x 20. The wood part was of a naturally finished oak but the wood section was also of other woods that were toned to simulate finishes. The compo part was generally gold in color. This pattern was applied to the wood by means of a cylindrical die. Most of the early runs of this material had very deep and sharp designs, but as time went by, the designs became shallow and thin. The basic wood part was semi-circular on top and the repair would be difficult because the conditions were similar to the shallow filigree design. It would be best to fake the design in, but time should be spent in that effort. By the use of spackle, a small camel hair brush, water and some patience, one can do a presentable job in faking in a missing piece.

The wood part of the frame can be restored, depending on the extent of work required. If the wood section was intact with little marring, then a wipe with a fruitwood stain could be helpful. If the wood part was in bad condition, then it would be advisable to strip the wood and refinish it. This type of frame can be taken apart since it is composed of perhaps three or four frames. It should be taken apart if the wood is to be stripped.

Refinishing Wood Frames

If it is determined that the wood frame should be stripped, then the following procedure should be used. If the frame is composed of many frame sections, then the frames should be separated. Apply a good paint remover to the surface. After a few minutes, remove what you can with steel wool. Repeat the operation until all the old finish is completely removed. It would be advisable to use gloves when using a paint remover. When you think that all the old finish has been removed, then apply one more coat and with the use of washing soda, scrub and wash the surface with the aid of steel wool. Finally, rinse it with fresh water and dry with toweling.

You cannot stain a wood without removing the old finish, because the stain will not adhere to the surface. Once the old finish is removed then you can apply a stain. Allow it to dry and then seal it with shellac and apply a finish coat. Some original oak frames were naturally finished. Through the years, a patina was created on the old finish. This was a thing of beauty since it was created with time. Duplicating the patina was no easy task. How does one begin to describe the orange amber dark tone of curly maple after fifty or seventy-five years and to say the least, duplicate it? Oak also takes on a patina of its own. To strip the wood and then to apply a finish will only result in an oak that has been recently finished. To come close to the patina, a combination of walnut and/or fruitwood stain can be helpful. Again, the author cannot say exactly what to do unless the exact conditions are known. He can only suggest the possible solutions to the problem.

Walnut is usually naturally finished. The wood has a small open grain which can be easily filled. Most of the restoration of walnut can be done by cleaning with soap and water. Sometimes many years of dirt accumulate on the top part of the frame and the bottom ledge. This soil and grease combination can get quite thick and hard. For this thick combination, a strong soap solution should be used.

If the finish is such that removal is necessary, then the same procedure for paint removal is followed. Normally the wood has a natural finish, but if a darker shade is wanted, then a walnut stain shall be used. Sometimes, by wiping the frame with walnut stain, this will freshen it it to a point where no other finishing is required and no finish removal is needed. A little paste wax should be used to top it off.

Pine was used to some extent in framing. The wood was used for compo application and also where whiting has been used to coat the wood. Pine does not take stains very well and its stability is not as good as the other woods used. Around 1890, yellow pine was used for the inexpensive wide and flat frame that housed the give-away pictures for soap coupons. The frame was about four inches wide and was covered with a compo that was rolled on with the cylindrical die. The material proved to be of poor quality with time. As time went by, the pine was affected by the elements and expansion followed contraction, resulting in the opening of the corners. Almost every frame of this type today requires work in closing up the corners. The solution of repair is the same as any compo corner repair. It would be advisable to add a little white glue to the spackle when filling in the corner. The glue gives the spackle a better grab on the frame and it sticks better.

Whether to Refinish the Whole Frame or Not

Sometimes the amount of repair is so extensive that the whole frame has to be refinished. If the frame has a fine appearance and the area is small then you should tone the repair part in with the procedure previously described in this book. If the repair is only needed to the edge of the frame, retone the entire outer edge, even though it is extensive. The object is to maintain as much of the patina of the original finish if that finish is attractive.

Some antique frames have finishes that are not attractive. Most of the gilt-finished frames have oxidized to a point that you would not like to hang them in your home. Black with gold had been done so that the item would be more acceptable for a funeral notice. In cases such as these it would be advisable to refinish the entire frame with tones that you prefer to use in the home. You may replace a velvet liner with a color that will blend with the picture and with the home.

XX – How to Tell If the Frame Is old

The art of faking antique objects goes back almost as far as the origins of the original articles. Sometimes when some article would be produced or created there would be someone who wanted to imitate that item and sell it cheaper. He would try to invent some other way that he could imitate it at less cost. Faking a duplicate is always done when it can be done cheaper. If producing the duplicate costs as much as the cost of the original, there will be little faking. With this fact in mind you can become aware if an item is fake through close examination, and by being equipped with certain facts, you will not be easily fooled.

Ovals

All early ovals in the 1800's were made of wood sections that were dovetailed together. No plywood was used. Although molded component compo parts are even used today, there were used extensively in the 1800's, and were very sharp with detail. The presence of real gold leaf is an indication of age and the gold leaf lip predominated. Watch for the joining distance between the sheets of leaf. If the distance is $5\frac{1}{2}$ inches it is imitation leaf, if the distance is $3\frac{1}{2}$ inches it is real gold leaf. Wide and deep ovals were of the earlier types. All ovals with a routed oblong back are old.

The most important factor is the condition of the back. One may go to extremes in trying to imitate an old frame on the face of the frame. It is possible to give the appearance of age to the face of the frame, but virtually no one will spend that much time trying to make the back look old. If they did and succeeded, then for heaven's sake buy the darn frame, because he has spent enough time on it! This rule applies to all frames: Look at the back and judge the frame. It should be soiled with age and possibly stained, banged up and also have indications of previous installations of pictures, etc.

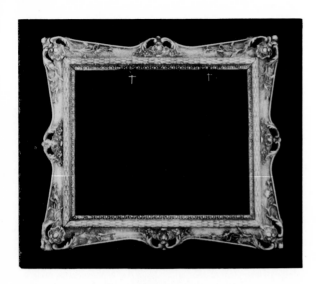

Figure 99
Circa 1895
size 16 by 20
Flat finished corner design all beading and trim by
compo mold, open network on corners, cylinder compo
on inner liner. Color gilt.

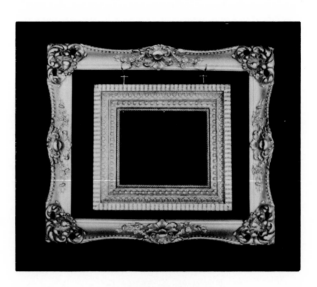

Figure 100
Circa 1895
size 16 by 20
Formed frame, compo mold corners and other parts.
Color, gold finish.

Figure 101

Inner frame
Circa 1885, size 8 by 10
Four frame, gold finish.

Figure 102
Circa 1910
Modified form frame, simple compo corners. Note
change from Fig. 100 by elimination of compo parts;
color, tiffany with gilt highlights.

Figure 103
Circa 1895
Three frame design, scalloped inner liner, cylinder compo outerframe, sometimes has added fourth outer simple
frame edging.

Compo Frames

The designs used on picture frames may go back as far as the thirteenth century. Combinations of compo and mouldings can also date back that far.

If the compo was applied from molds to the surface of the frame then it is an indication that the frame is old. You can tell by spotting the joining of the short compo pieces. A frame with a lot of molded decorations indicates age, as do detailed sections and especially pieces that would have difficulty in being released from the mold.

The wood part of the frame can tell you something of its age. If a corner fastener was used the frame is not old. If the frame is only one inch thick but it is on a concave angle then the frame is usually not old, although frames with tortoise shell finish did appear around 1900 that match this description. If the wood section is built up to greater than one inch then the frame may have age, but not necessarily so. If the frame has hairline cracks in it, the frame is old. If the design has the acorn and oak leaf pattern in it the frame is probably old. Remember to look at the back of the frame for age signs.

Natural Wood Frames

Walnut frames with dimension and character are probably old. Oak frames will be wide, flat or with some contour to them. There will usually be a patina to the finish of the oak which was either finished in black, English oak, or natural which was amber with age. The antique frame usually had a fine ornamental liner with it. The liner could be a simple gold leaf or compo covered with a design. The liners would have obvious age to them. Distressed frames do not necessarily mean old frames. This type of finish is done easily. Again, look at the back of the frame to determine the age.

Multi-framed Picture Frames

Any frame that is composed of many frame units usually is from the 1800's and early 1900's. By the fact of cost alone this practice was discontinued in the early 1900's. The practice of making one complete frame was the trend after 1900.

When Is a Frame an Antique?

The general accepted view is that an item must be 100 years old to be an antique, or that items prior to 1865 shall be considered antique.

The author believes this to be an arbitrary date and not in line with reality. For the sake of a date I have chosen 1900 as a line of frame antiquity, not ignoring the 1900-1915 era as antique in the sense that what was antique in 1900 was also antique in 1915 if the same basic design was used. From 1900 there began a transition period to different frames which has been described before in other parts of this book. In dating frames of this period involved I allow a ten-year leeway one way or the other since a certain frame design does not first appear in 1880, then disappear in 1881. The stock could, perhaps, be used until 1900 or so. The predominant period, however, was approximately 1880.

XIX — Where Can We Find the Antique Frame?

Pictures frames were one of the most neglected items in antiquity. Because of the recent trend toward simplicity there was no demand at all for the antique frames. Unlike antiques in general the frame was still a component of a picture unit. A small antique vase could be put on a shelf, but unless you put a picture in the frame, it could not be used. Since it hung on the wall, the picture unit affected the decor of the room.

Figure 104

Circa 1880
size 14 by 17
Four frame design. Oak feature liner, sterling silver
on cylinder compo, portrait type frame.

Figure 105

Circa 1885
size 16 by 20
Four frame design, sterling silver on compo, black
velvet feature liner, portrait frame.

Figure 106

Circa 1885
size 16 by 20
Five frame design, very wide, ivory and gilt gold,
combination cylinder and mold compo.

Figure 107

Circa 1895
size 16 by 20
Typical portrait frame, oak and gold, gold simulated silver liner. Four frame construction.

Demand for this style was not present and the frame was destined to fade into oblivion.

When each generation dies, the belongings of that generation usually come on the market. House auctions were the main source of frames. Because of the lack of interest, many a bundle of frames were sold for a dollar or simply burned up at the end of the auction. Not a day goes by when someone does not tell me of how they threw out this frame or that frame.

Frames simply accumlated in the antique shops and were sold for fifty cents up to maybe two dollars. Most of the frames required work, because they were neglected. Stored in attics, barns and damp basements, the elements took their toll.

One of the biggest destroyers of frames were the hooks on the backs of the frames. They stuck out and when they were stacked on another frame, they gouged and scratched the frames they rested on. It is most disheartening to see a beautiful tortoise frame gouged out because of these hooks. Antique dealers, I implore you to remove the hooks when you pick up frames. They are very inexpensive to replace and the wire is probably rotten anyway.

Practically all the early frames west of the Mississippi River came from east of the Mississippi. With the exception of St. Louis, most frames were made in the east. Today, and for the last few years, the demand for antique frames has increased. California and Texas buyers were stripping as much antique material as they could find in east Illinois which, being the closest state, was the first to be stripped. Indiana and Wisconsin soon followed. As the buyers penetrated further east, Ohio became next, and finally Pennsylvania and New York State. Van loads after van loads of antiques were taken out of these states. It seemed that the supply was endless, but it was not. When one realizes that over 200 million people now live in America—and I believe that less than one million frames now exist —this means less than one frame for each 200 persons, and considering conditions of the frames, less than one frame in perfect condition for each 1000 persons.

Some people have felt that the south would be a mecca for frames, but this is not true. Shortly after the Civil War, the south was literally stripped of every conceivable commodity that could be bartered or carried away. In a very short time nothing of value was left. Eventually, the antique dealer for want of merchandise, penetrated into southern Illinois, Kentucky, southern Ohio, Indiana and the southern part of Pennsylvania. Practically all of the antiques and frames in the southern antique markets came from elsewhere.

There was a severe shortage of antique frames in Chicago due to the bonfire known as the Chicago fire. Most of the frames were burned up.

As I have mentioned before, the western and southern buyers were taking van load after van load out of the central and eastern states. Maine and New Hampshire was also being cleaned out. As the antique frame disappeared, the demand increased, partially due to the upsurge in art. People were beginning to realize the importance of the frame to the picture. Now these frames are few and far between. Antique dealers can now boast of only a few hanging in their shops. The beautiful gems are gone.

Another situation has been occurring that effects the antique dealers in their supply. For a long time people known as "pickers" have supplied the dealers with their supply. The picker was usually a person well known and well liked in the community. They had the opportunity to get into barns, attics, etc., and purchase items that the people wished to sell. This material was then sold to the antique dealer.

Today, because of the antique shortage, some pickers now bypass the

Figure 108

Empire style mirror, Circa 1812-
1850, wood frame, eagle holding
flag is painted on glass, mercury
mirror,

antique dealer and go directly to the auctions where the dealer is now forced to compete for items with the general public. Prices soon reach new highs because a retail market is reached there. Many an item cannot be bought by the dealer simply because there is no room for profit and that profit is rightfully theirs. Virtually every commodity, be it picture frame or sofa, has to have a supplier, a wholesaler, and a dealer structure to sell to the public. Each level contributes something to the public. The supplier, which is the home where it came from, can be personally reached by the wholesaler, who is the picker. The picker does not have a store operation, but instead has a car, truck or van out of which he or she operates. The antique dealer has the store or place of operation. They perform the service because they have the selection, the variety and the reliability of a base of operations. The public can go to them regularly. Certain items that you may seek may be found with their help. When you bypass the antique dealer, you actually are cutting off their supply. Each year hundreds of dealers are going out of business, not because there is no business, but because there is no supply.

Another reason for this situation lies in Flea Market or garage sale operations. In the garage sale, the people who would normally sell to the picker or antique dealer, now sells to the public. In the flea market, many of the people who rent a space there are pickers who, for a few dollars on a Sunday, can also sell directly to the public. One can well understand why there are some bad feelings here. The antique dealer is solving some of this by using the adage: "If you can't beat 'em, join 'em." More and more antique dealers are appearing at flea markets. There are so many dealers now that these markets are called "Antique Flea Markets." It then gives the dealer a chance to pick up items for their resale. These are the items that normally came to them from the picker. Now let me make this perfectly clear; we need the antique dealers. If they disappear, the public will someday find that there is no place to go for service when one is looking for the items they collect. There is no reliable base of operations. Let us support our local dealers.

Practically everything of unique value on the retail market is gone. Go to the average antique show and you will, perhaps, see two frames. This indicates how many they probably have in their shops. For the time being the only places where frames may exist in any quantity to be purchased are house sales, remaining old homes that may be untouched and flea markets away from major centers of population. The flea market operations in small towns will make some materials available.

As for states that have material, I believe New York State and Ohio still have frames available in some quantity, again away from major cities such as Cleveland, Pittsburgh and New York City. Auctions will produce frames, but they will not be cheap, because you bid against competition.

One has to understand the definition of a "decent buy." If the frame is intact and no repair needed, then you can establish price by its replacement value and then add to it the antique value. If repairs are needed, there is considerable depreciation in value, because of the labor cost to repair the frame—if you can find someone reliable to do the job. Good restorers are hard to find. Anyone can fill a spot with spackle, but to do a good job, a casting of the missing part should be done. This requires a considerable amount of skill, but if the frame is a good one, it is worth it!

Help to preserve this beautiful object of beauty that is leaving us slowly. If you have frames now, please preserve them, hand them down to your children. Inform them of the history of the frames, and see that these objects live on and on and on.

INDEX